Logic

FOR

CHRISTIANS

———

Critical Thinking
for the People of God

———

zach lee

LUCIDBOOKS

Logic for Christians
Critical Thinking for the People of God

Copyright © 2021 by Zach Lee

Published by Lucid Books in Houston, TX
www.lucidbookspublishing.com

ISBN: 978-1-63296-438-0
eISBN: 978-1-63296-439-7

Special Sales: Most Lucid Books titles are available in special quantity discounts. Custom imprinting or excerpting can also be done to fit special needs. For standard bulk orders, go to www.lucidbooksbulk.com. For specialty press or large orders, contact Lucid Books at books@lucidbookspublishing.com.

table of contents

special thanks

Many people helped make this book possible. Without them, it would never have made it to production. I offer special thanks to:

The staff of The Parkway Church who motivated me, read the original manuscript, and offered helpful advice along the way. Though I'm prone to depression and anxiety, their friendship has always been a source of encouragement.

The pastors and elders of The Parkway Church who prayed for me, encouraged me, and graciously allowed me to engage in this project as a resource for our congregation and for others who might find it helpful.

The many anonymous financial donors, both at our church and elsewhere, who sacrificially gave so that the initial funding for the book could be raised.

My professors, both in the fields of philosophy and theology, who instilled in me a love of logic, debate, and coherent thinking and who taught me that logic is a tool to assist us in better knowing God's word.

The incredible team at Lucid Books who held my hand through this process. Their kindness and professionalism made the publishing process a joy.

And, most importantly, my sweet wife, Katy. She knows the worst parts of me, and yet she loves me anyway. I dedicate this book to her. This is a book on learning how to reason and, as John Nash tells his wife in the movie *A Beautiful Mind*, "You are all my reasons."

PART I

a little logic

CHAPTER 1

what is logic?

Astudent walked into a philosophy professor's office at a local community college and said, "I'm interested in taking your course on logic; I just don't know what logic is." The professor smiled and said, "That's not a problem; I'll show you." The professor continued, "I assume that you have at least one child. Am I correct in my assumption?" Astounded, the student asked, "How did you know that?" "Well," said the professor, "I used a little logic. I saw that you had grass stains on your shoes, which led me to conclude that you most likely have a lawn. And if you have a lawn, then you most likely have a house. And if you have a house at your age (and by the fact that you are wearing a wedding ring), then I assume you are probably married. And since you look to be in your late thirties, I assume that you probably have kids as well."

Blown away, the student signed up for the course and headed back to work. During lunch he told one of his coworkers that he was going to take a logic class at the local community college. "What is logic?" his coworker asked. "Well," he responded, "I'll show you. Do you have any grass stains on your shoes?" "No," replied the co-worker. The student replied, "Then I assume you must hate kids."

This fictional story shows how our thinking can go astray.

Every one of us believes something that is false. We believe many things that are inconsistent with other things we believe. We all make mistakes in our reasoning, and we do it on a daily basis. We might use words incorrectly, believe false things that we have been told by authority figures, or be biased in our thinking by our experience, upbringing, or culture. We might commit logical fallacies or misunderstand the very position for which we are advocating.

To become better thinkers, we must learn a little about logic. Logic allows us to put ideas together in a way that is clear, consistent, and helpful. It allows us, like Sherlock Holmes, to come to correct conclusions about the world around us by seeing how everything fits together.

What Makes This Book Unique?

First, I have written this book primarily for Christians who want to become better thinkers. To be fair, a non-Christian can still benefit greatly from the information given within these pages. Regardless of your worldview, I hope you will give it a try. But I have intentionally written this for Christians and have, therefore, used a lot of biblical and theological topics in my examples, fallacies, and arguments.

Second, I have written this book at a layperson's level. I have intentionally avoided a lot of technical jargon and some advanced concepts such as probability calculus and advanced symbolic logic (which I had to drudge through when I was studying logic in grad school).[1] I have avoided technical definitions, conversations on how logical theory has changed (from Boethius, Boole, Frege, Russell, and others), and most topics that would make you want to fall asleep. Halfway through my second logic course, I realized that all the technical stuff I was learning would not be used by 99 percent of the students in the class. The technical stuff is important. But it is not that important for the average Christian who just wants to think more clearly. I have intentionally kept this book short. But the price for keeping it short is that you will have to read it slowly. I've packed big ideas into short sentences, so feel free to slow down and reread if necessary.

Third, I have written it in a playful tone throughout. I make fun of several theological positions (even my own); I have included little jokes in certain sections and have tried to make learning logic as enjoyable as I can. I hope no one will be offended by my tone, mockery, sarcasm, and silliness and will instead see it as my attempt to take something that is usually dry and dull and make it entertaining. I also understand that some of the topics addressed are controversial (especially in the second half of the book). My intent is not to be harsh, condemning, or unloving. This is a book on logic, so I cannot get into every nuance of every theological, social, and political issue I address. After all, seeing where our thinking goes astray can help produce humility. As the famous playwright, Molière, remarked centuries ago:

> The mission of comedy is to correct men's vices . . .
> most men are scolded by nothing quite so well as by
> the portrayal of their faults. It is a great blow to vice
> to expose it to everyone's laughter. We can easily
> stand being reprehended, but we cannot stand being
> mocked.[2]

Finally, I have spent most of the book discussing logical fallacies, especially as they relate to arguments that Christians make for different theological and ethical positions. This allows us to take a subject that can be somewhat sterile and make it a little spicier. Most logic books have a short chapter or section on logical fallacies, but I devote about half of this book to the subject. Why is that? Well, I have found that students retain information better if they work through real-life issues and are given examples of bad reasoning.

Though this book could serve as supplemental reading for a student at a Christian college or seminary, my aim is to help the average Christian in their thinking. Christianity is not primarily an experiential religion but a propositional religion. Don't get me wrong; it does involve experience. But it is founded on propositional truth. God is a Trinity. Jesus is Lord. Christ was raised from the dead. God saves by grace. Christ is coming back. All these propositions (and many more!) show how much our faith is founded on whether certain claims are true in reality. With all this in mind we are ready to ask, "What is logic?"

Logic

Logic is a way to help us think critically and clearly. It comes from the Greek word *logos*, which just means "word," but also relates to the notions of argument, reasoning, and truth. But what exactly is logic, and why do we need it?

There are many definitions of logic. Some define it as "the study of the methods and principles used to distinguish correct from incorrect reasoning."[3] Others define logic as "the science that evaluates arguments."[4] Some, like Immanuel Kant, define it abstractly as "the form of thought."[5] Reportedly, Alvin Plantinga, professor of philosophy at the University of Notre Dame, often quips that logic is simply thinking really hard about something. And others avoid technical definitions altogether and simply call it "clear and effective thinking."[6]

If I were to have a go at defining logic, I would say that it is simply working out the implications of the notion of absolute truth.

But no definition is fully satisfactory because logic is not like any other subject. Logic is the subject that stands over every other subject. *It is the subject that you have to take for granted before you can make a truth claim in any other field.* Take biology, for example. In biology you might cut open a frog in eighth-grade science class and look at the frog's heart (while also trying to gross out the girl sitting beside you). Or you might try to create some genetically modified plant, Gregor Mendel-style. Or you might look at red blood cells under a microscope. In biology, you are standing above your subject (living things) to study them.

Logic, however, doesn't work that way. You don't stand over logic; logic stands over you. Logic, a subset of philosophy, is all about evaluating arguments and, therefore, is foundational for all other modes of inquiry. Philosophy asks questions such as, "What even is a frog, and how do we know? Is it ethical to cut them open? And how do we know that the frog that I'm seeing with my eyes is the same as the frog that is actually on the table?" When someone says, "This frog is dead," logic asks, "What reasons can you give me for that claim, and are they sound?"

Logic is the foundation for other disciplines. Before one can say that "water freezes at 32°F," one has to have rules for what does and does not count as proof for this claim. Logic is about argumentation. It is about saying something true and then using reasons to prove that it is true. It is about evaluating when someone says something false and showing how they made a logical misstep or how the reasons they gave do not support what they are claiming. Logic gets a say in politics, theology, economics, biology, math, and every other discipline. If you are making a claim, then you are doing logic (either well or poorly).

We live in a society that doesn't study logic. Though logic was a mandatory subject in school for most of Western history, most students today are not taught logic until college and, even then, most don't study it as part of their degree program. Most students simply want to get their diploma so they can get a job and make money. Learning to think has taken a back seat to getting a piece of paper to add to a resume. Ironically, even saying the sentence, "I want to get an education to make money," is itself a proposition and deals with logic. Giving reasons for why you want to make money (to have a big house, fancy car, etc.) is making an argument by using logic.

Logic is concerned with things such as propositions and arguments. Now, let me define those terms briefly. A proposition is merely a sentence that makes a claim. It is an indicative sentence. Not all sentences are propositions, but all propositions are sentences. Let me give some examples:

Sentences that are not propositions:

"Why do I have to get my back waxed?"

"Get on the ground, scumbag!"

"Let us eat as much Jello as possible."

Notice that all of these are sentences, but they are not all propositions. The first is a question (an interrogative), the second is a command (an imperative), and the third, in addition to being a strange sentence, is what is pretentiously known as a "hortatory subjunctive."

Sentences that are propositions:

> "Tacos are like burgers, only sideways."
>
> "You should not vote for that candidate."
>
> "Pastor Bob is really weird."

These are all sentences, but they are also propositions because they all make a claim. They contain a subject about which they are saying something.

In logic we are primarily concerned with propositions.

Now let's define an argument. Don't get tricked on this one. In our culture people use the term *argument* to mean anything that is a verbal dispute (like when you fight with your spouse over who left the cap off the toothpaste). To most people, the word *argument* has a negative connotation. But in logic an argument is simply where you give reasons for why you believe what you believe.

Allow me to say something that may be a bit hard to hear although it is true, and we will see why it is true later:

> *You don't have a right to your opinion. You only have a right to what you can argue for.[7] And your arguments must be good ones.*

Argument is how you support your proposition with reasons. If you say, "Christians should practice infant baptism," that is a proposition that you have to support with arguments. Conversely, if you say, "Christians should practice believer's baptism," that is a proposition that you have to support with arguments.

Finally, there is no getting away from logic or acting like you can just ignore it. In fact, you even need logic to try to deny logic.

Let that sink in for a second. Even if someone says, "You don't need logic," they have made a proposition (that is either true or false) and must give reasons for why they believe that claim. There is no "not-doing-logic." We do it all the time. My aim for this book is that we might be able to do it better. We are all logicians; the question is whether we will be good ones.

absolute truth

W e live in a world that has an allergy to truth:

"That's just your opinion."

"What's true for you is true for you, and what is true for me is true for me."

"Each person should live their own truth."

"Listen to your heart."

These, and other phrases like these, permeate social media, the news, classrooms, and workplaces across the country.

But are they right? Is truth true for everyone? Some? None? Is there such a thing as absolute truth?

Believe it or not the idea of truth that is true for everyone is embedded into the very fabric of all rational discourse. All coherent thinking assumes that truth exists. Imagine, for example, that someone were to support the idea that "all crows are black." Now, if it turned out that all crows were indeed black, then they would be right. However, since not all crows are black (there are albino crows, by the way), then that sentence is false. It's not just false for them. It is false *in reality*. What kind of crows there are in the actual world has absolutely nothing to do with what individuals believe about crows. It is something objective, not subjective (even if everyone in the world were to disagree with it).

This is the Christian notion of truth. It is what is called the "correspondence theory of truth." When a claim matches up with reality, that is truth. When a claim does not match up with reality, that is falsehood. If there is a cat sitting on a mat and I say, "There is a cat sitting on a mat," my words have lined up with reality and are therefore true. If there is a cat sitting on the mat and I say, "There is *not* a cat sitting on the mat," my words have *not* lined up with reality and are therefore false. This is also the definition of truth given in a famous dictum by Aristotle: "To say of what is that it is, and of what is not that it is not, is true."[1]

Now, here is something that may shock you: This idea of truth is not just some "Christian version of truth." It is the way reality actually works. If an atheist claims that "there is no God," and in reality, there is no God, then he is right! He is being honest; he is speaking truth. However, if an atheist claims that "there is no God," and in reality, there is a God, then he is wrong. He is being dishonest; he is speaking a falsehood. Truth is not just a "religious" thing. Truth is an undeniable facet of the way things are in reality, regardless of one's worldview.

Notice that "truth" and "absolute truth" are the same thing. This sounds like a controversial claim in postmodern, Western societies, but it is basic common sense for the rest of humanity (and has been for nearly all of world history).

Think about the odd conclusions you run into if you deny absolute truth and embrace relativism. For example, if someone who is a flat-earther (someone who, despite the overwhelming evidence of science, believes that the earth is flat) said, "The world is flat," a relativist would have to say that claim was *true for them*. But if someone who believes the earth is round (as I do) says, "The world is round," a relativist would have to say that claim was *true for them*. How can both of those statements be true *at the same time*? Nobody cares whether it is "true for them" or "true for me." We want to know *in reality* whether the earth is round or flat.

Or imagine that someone was a Holocaust-denier (someone who, despite the overwhelming evidence of history, believes the Holocaust never happened). If you don't believe in absolute truth and you think all truth is relative, you would have to say that the phrase "The Holocaust never happened" *was true for the person making that claim*. To hold that position is not only illogical. It is absolutely insane.[2]

You see, if someone doesn't believe in absolute truth, then they can't even say that the sentence "There is no such thing as absolute truth" is true. They are just stuck logically contradicting themselves (and looking a bit silly) at every turn. When someone says, "There is no such thing as absolute truth," I simply ask them, "Are you sure?" If they say no, then I let them know that absolute truth might exist (after all, if they are not sure they are right, then they might be wrong). If they say yes, they have shown that there is at least one absolute truth—namely, the absolute truth of the sentence: "There is no such thing as absolute truth." Saying there is no absolute truth is like someone saying, "I don't exist," and thinking that they are right in that claim. If you don't exist, who is speaking that sentence?

When I hear people try to defend the idea that there is no

such thing as absolute truth, they never seem to realize the irony of what they are doing. *If you really didn't believe in absolute truth, you surely could not make a case for it.* As soon as you use any words, arguments, or sentences, you are showing that you implicitly believe in absolute truth. No one can be a consistent relativist and stay alive for more than a few minutes. If someone is walking into oncoming traffic and I say, "Watch out!" they will not yell back, "That's just your truth; getting hit by trucks won't hurt me."

But we don't have to prove that there is such a thing as absolute truth by showing the logical contradictions of those who deny it. We can show examples of absolutely true statements that are factually certain.

Let's consider a few examples of sentences that are true:

Suppose I write the sentence "I exist." This sentence is absolutely true at the time I write it. Not only is it true (I am, after all, the one who typed this sentence), it *cannot* be false. The claim, "I exist," is self-authenticating. One cannot make that claim unless they do in fact exist. Even if you *try* to say that I'm wrong, then I've still shown an example of absolute truth because a non-existing thing cannot be wrong![3] When a person says, "I exist," they are making an absolute truth claim. This is the strongest type of claim. Not only is it true in reality (metaphysically), but I can also personally *know* it is true (epistemologically).

Or consider statements such as "All bachelors are unmarried" or "A triangle has three sides" or "Two plus two equals four." These also are absolutely true. They are deductively and intuitively true (more on this in a later chapter). But absolute truth doesn't just pertain to these deductive types of mathematically precise statements. There are a lot of statements that are absolutely true.

For example, I might say:

> "There are no 10,000-pound giant pink tigers in my
> living room."

That is an absolute truth. It doesn't matter what you think about it. It doesn't matter what I think about it. It is true. Now, you can make the claim that I could be deceived or that I'm dreaming or that I cannot prove my claim, but all that would do is claim that I *might* be wrong. But think about what your claim does. If I *might be wrong,* then the sentence "Zach might be wrong" would be true, thus proving that absolute truth exists.

You cannot get away from absolute truth because it is an element of logic. It is a truth that is hardwired into the universe. *You even need absolute truth to try to deny absolute truth.* The sentence "There is absolute truth" is either true (and hence it exists), or it is false, which also means that there is absolute truth because its falsity would be absolutely true.

That's some proof from the logical side. Now for the theological side.

If you are a Christian, you are bound to hold to absolute truth. It is not an option for you. The entire Christian faith is based on the fact that God's truth is binding on all people. It's not just that some people need Jesus; all people do. You cannot say that Jesus being the eternal Son of God is true for you but not true for me. If you are a Christian, you must say that this claim is absolutely true. You cannot hold that the command not to steal is true for you but not true for me. You cannot hold that the Bible is God's word for you but not for me. You cannot say that sexual immorality is okay for you but not for me. Christianity presupposes the idea of absolute truth. If someone interprets a passage of scripture correctly, then they are honoring God. If someone misinterprets a passage of scripture, then they are dishonoring God. Christianity is all about truth. It is about believing what is right.

Have you ever had someone criticize you for trying to be "right"? Why is wanting to be right a bad thing? Shouldn't we seek to be right in every area of life? Doesn't God call us to hold the right views about him, his word, salvation, and morality? Yes, we should be kind, and yes, we should be sensitive, and yes, we are commanded to speak the truth in love. But our loving tone should *go along with* our truth and not to the exclusion of it. *You cannot hold a falsehood to the glory of God.*

Philosopher and theologian Phillip Cary says,

> The love of truth means that we want reality to rule our hearts. It is based on a deep and rather extraordinary optimism that says ignorance is not bliss, because ultimately the truth about reality is the best news of all. It's an optimism that hardly makes sense at all unless God is Truth. What is most fundamentally sad about the effort to prevent people from thinking too much is that it means giving up this optimism. It means being afraid that questions, followed honestly, lead to evil, because the search for truth ultimately leads away from God.[4]

But whether you believe in absolute truth from Christianity or from the philosophical proofs given above, one thing is clear: You cannot disagree with me (i.e., think I'm wrong) and also deny absolute truth. If you deny absolute truth, you're stuck keeping your logically incoherent views to yourself.

CHAPTER 3

the laws of logic

I once heard someone who was in an argument say to their opponent, "Well, that's just *your* logic." Wait a second. *Your* logic? I have no idea what on earth they were trying to say by uttering that hopelessly strange and unintelligible sentence. That is kind of like saying, "That's just *your* math," or "That's just *your* geometry," or "That's just *your* absolute, binding, objective, universal fact."

Logic is not subjective. It is objective. Logic deals with rules that apply to everyone. There is no such thing as "old people's logic" or "white people's logic" or "tall people's logic" or "poor people's logic." Logic is not part of one culture. It is part of reality for all cultures.

There are a lot of rules when it comes to logic. But logic itself is really based on just a handful of "logical axioms." A logical axiom is a necessary truth that is the bedrock on which we build everything else. It is not supported by other arguments because it needs no support. It is immediately and obviously true. As soon as someone hears a logical axiom, it is intuitively and clearly true. For our purposes, we will state three logical axioms that will carry us through the rest of the book.

1. The law of non-contradiction – Something cannot both *be* and *not be* at the same time in the same way.
2. The law of identity – Whatever is, is. Whatever is not, is not.
3. The law of the excluded middle – Everything must either be or not be.

Now, that sounds kind of technical with all that "being" language, so let me say it in a way that doesn't sound like I got stuffed into a locker for being a geek in high school.

The law of non-contradiction means that something cannot be both true and false (in the same way) at the exact same time. I can say that "I'm hungry" and later say that "I'm not hungry," but I can't say, "I am both hungry and not hungry right now," and mean the same thing by the word *hungry* in both senses. Sure, I can utter those words, but I can't make it mean anything in reality.

The second law simply means that true things are indeed true, and false things are indeed false. That's pretty obvious. True things are true, and false things are false. You see why these rules are axioms and don't need further proof. They are intuitively and obviously true.

The third law simply means that all *propositions* are either true or false. The sentence "Abraham Lincoln had a beard on May 21, 1862, at 5:32 p.m." is either true or false, but it is not both. It must be one or the other. Even if we don't *know* whether it is true or false, it still is true or false in reality. Even if nobody was around Abraham Lincoln on that day (and didn't know whether he shaved his beard), it is still either true or false. *A truth does not require that humans believe that it is true for it to be true.*

But here is the good news. You don't have to remember all this. You only have to remember the first law, the law of non-contradiction, because the other two laws flow forth from it.

The Biggest Rule of Logic: Don't Break the Law of Non-contradiction

The first law, the law of non-contradiction, simply states that if something is true, it cannot be false at the same time. For example, if I say, "Jesus is Lord," I cannot mean "Jesus is not Lord" if all my terms retain their same meaning. Those two claims contradict each other. I cannot put my hand on a table and say, "This is a table, and this is also not a table," and mean the same thing by all my words. If I did, that would make absolutely no sense.

Notice how we see that this is obviously true. I cannot both affirm something and deny something while meaning the same thing by that "something." The law of non-contradiction is not something I can prove by going back further. We see that it is *self-proving*. It is where we start. It doesn't have a further foundation; it is the foundation. It must be true. All absolute truth is built on the idea of non-contradiction.

To prove my point, stop reading this sentence and try to think of something that breaks the law of non-contradiction. Try to think of something that both *is* and *is not* at the exact same time and *in the exact same way.*

If you are already reading this sentence, then you have not taken enough time to think about it. Really try hard. I'll wait. . . .

You cannot do it. Now, you may be thinking that you did, but I assure you, you did not. If you think you did, then you accidentally changed the meaning of one of your terms. But if you keep your terms the same, it cannot be done. If you could break the law of non-contradiction, then you could also not break the law of non-contradiction at the same time. *You even need the law of non-contradiction to try to disprove the law of non-contradiction.*

It's important to note that an actual contradiction means that all your words retain their same meaning throughout your sentence. If you change the meaning of your words, things will become confused.

Let's consider two examples:

First, let's assume I declare, "I both do and also do not exist." That is a contradiction. It breaks the first law of logic. It is absolutely nonsense. You see? The law of non-contradiction works!

But let's look at a second example. Let's say I point to my three-year-old son and say, "He is a man, and he is not a man." Now, if by the word *man* I mean the exact same thing throughout the sentence, then I have broken the law of non-contradiction.

But there is a way in which that sentence can be true depending on what I mean by the word *man*. Perhaps by the first use of the word *man*, I meant "male," and by the second use of the word *man*, I meant "fully grown adult." In the first use of the word, the contrast is about gender (male as opposed to female). In the second use of the word, the contrast is about age (adult as opposed to boy). I would then be saying that my son is a man in the sense that he is male, but he is not a man in the sense that he is just a little boy. That is not breaking the law of non-contradiction *because I have changed the meaning of the word* "man." If you keep your terms the same, the law of non-contradiction works every time, without exception. However, if you change your terms, then there is no longer a contradiction. Most alleged contradictions in the

Bible are not really contradictions. They are instances in which the meaning of a word has changed based upon the context (but more on this in "Part II – Logical Fallacies").

Everything we say, everything we think, and everything the Bible says is built upon the law of non-contradiction. When the Bible says, "Do not commit adultery," it cannot also mean that you should commit adultery. When the Bible says that "David killed Goliath," it cannot also mean that he did not kill Goliath. All meaning is built upon the idea that something does not imply its logical opposite. This holds for every worldview. Even someone who says, "I don't believe in the law of non-contradiction," cannot also mean "I fully believe in the law of non-contradiction" at the same time.

You should be seeing a theme emerge. Truth, absolute truth, and the law of non-contradiction are really the same thing. They are all pointing to the fact that a true contradiction is impossible. Let's end this chapter with a little logic puzzle to further make the point.

Is the following sentence true or false?

"This sentence is false."

Think about it for a second. What is your answer?

If you say that the sentence, "This sentence is false," is indeed *true*, then it must be false because it honestly declares itself to be false. But if the sentence, "This sentence is false," is *false*, then it must be true again (because if it's false that it's false, then it's true—two negations make an affirmation). This would make it false again, which would make it true again, and on and on we could go. Is your head spinning yet?

The answer to the puzzle is to realize that the sentence, "This sentence is false," is not really a sentence at all. It is a bunch of words parading around like a sentence, but it is actually a logical contradiction. It is breaking the law of non-contradiction, which is why we cannot answer whether it is true or false. It claims to be true, and it claims to be false in the same way at the same time.

We must keep in mind that a logical contradiction is literally *impossible*. We also have to keep in mind that we often use sentences in ways that are not proper. Not all sentences are really "sentences." Some sentences are linguistic wolves in propositions' clothing. They seem like sentences, but they are not:

> "This sentence is false" contains words but doesn't actually claim anything. It is not a real sentence.

> "Were isn't betwixt Ned on couches green" contains words, but it is not a real sentence.

> "A an and any an Andy A" contains words but is not a real sentence.

> "I am both thinking about and not thinking about this sentence at the same time" contains words but is not a real sentence.

Remember this the next time you hear someone presenting an argument. Christians sometimes make this mistake in theology. I've heard people say, "Perhaps God both does and doesn't elect people." That is a non-sentence if they mean the same thing by the word *elect*.

But what about this famous logic puzzle:

> "Can God make a rock so big he cannot move it?"

To answer that, we have to look at our next chapter on how God relates to logic.

CHAPTER 4

god and logic

L et's begin by asking a popular question that was debated a lot in the Middle Ages:

"Is something good because God declares that it is 'good,' or does God declare it 'good' because it already is good?"

When the Bible says that murder is bad, is it because it is inherently bad, or is it only bad because God says, "Thou shall not murder"? Could God have made the world such that murder (not justified killing, but murder) was okay?

There is not an easy answer to this question. If you say God *had* to say that murder was bad, then it seems like God is bound to command things a certain way, and he could not have commanded them in any other way—meaning that God had no right to choose to command things differently than he did. This view seems to severely limit the way God could have created both the world and mankind. But if you say murder is only bad because God says it's bad, then the morality that God prescribes begins to look a bit arbitrary. Could God have commanded us to sexually assault one another and, therefore, assault would have been a good act?

Well, sorry to disappoint you, but we won't be able to answer this question here. *Womp Womp.* That is a question for theology, and it is beyond the bounds of this short book. However, I bring it up because it is related to another question that directly ties into logic.

When we say, "God is good," what do we mean by that sentence? Do we mean that there is some category that stands above God called "good" to which God must submit?

I would suggest that when we say that God is good, all we are really saying is that God is God. We know what good is because it is something that conforms to the character of God, not the other way around. So, goodness is not a standard that exists above God, to which he is subject but is rather an attribute of God's nature. What God does, by nature, is good. When we call anything else good, we are saying that it conforms to the will of God. God is the standard of goodness. He does not submit to a higher standard.

So, our conclusion thus far is this: Good simply means what corresponds with God's character and will; it is not some standard above God to which he must submit.

The same thing is true when we say that God is love. This does not mean that we bow down and worship a Valentine's Day card. It also does not mean that there is some standard called "love" that is above God. Rather, when we say that God is love, we are saying that God is God. We know what love is because it is something that conforms to God's character, not the other way around.

I believe the same thing is true about logic. God is logical. Logic is one of God's attributes. He is powerful, merciful, wrathful, loving, and logical. He has to be. When the Bible teaches that it is impossible for God to lie (Heb. 6:18), this means that when God makes a claim, he follows the law of non-contradiction. He does not contradict himself (which is what a lie is). He cannot say he will do one thing and not do it, or else he has broken the law of non-contradiction.

This is not because logic stands over God but because logic is a part of God's nature (like the example of goodness above). When we say that God is good, we really mean that we know what goodness is because of God's nature. When we say that God is logical, we really mean that we know what logic is because of God's nature.

So, to say it in a really deep way: *Logic is logical because it conforms to God.*

God is consistent in his actions. He doesn't contradict himself. What he says is true, and its opposite is false. God is logical and always truthful.

Now, with that in mind, let's ask a tricky question. Can God himself break the law of non-contradiction? Can God act in a way that is illogical? Now, to be clear, I don't mean, "Can God act in a way that seems illogical from our point of view?" He does that all the time. God's ways are not our ways, so we can't judge him by what we think is reasonable (defined by our limited human understanding). But that's not what I'm asking. *I'm asking whether God can break the law of non-contradiction. Can God do a logical impossibility?* I'm also not asking whether he can do what we consider to be a physical impossibility; he does that all the time: raising the dead, multiplying loaves and fish, healing the sick, etc. In that sense miracles are not truly impossible because they can happen. But can God do a logical impossibility? Can he make a square circle while the words *square* and *circle* mean exactly what they do today? Can he make two plus two equal five? Can God lie and not lie at the same time?

Throughout most of church history, the answer to this question has been an emphatic "No." God cannot break the law of non-contradiction. If he did, what would that even mean?

Not being able to break the law of non-contradiction is not a weakness on God's part because *breaking the law of non-contradiction is not a thing*. It doesn't exist. God is not weak if I say God can't "slkjflnksd" because "slkjflnksd" is not a thing; it's just a bunch of random letters that I typed. The same is true with breaking the law of non-contradiction. If God could break that law, then he could take away your salvation and not take it away at the same time. He could cease to be God. He could lie, and it could also be impossible for him to lie. You see, if God could break this law, he would not be God.

Before you freak out about the fact that I just said there is something that God cannot do, notice that the Bible already teaches this truth. God cannot lie (Heb. 6:18). He cannot cease to be God. He cannot change (Mal. 3:6; Ps.102:25–27; Heb. 6:17–18; James 1:17). He cannot decide to no longer be a Trinity. We have to realize that this is not because God is limited or weak; it is because all these things are, themselves, *weaknesses*. They are *privations*. When someone says, "God can't lie," we have to remember that lying is not a strength but a weakness. It is like saying, "God isn't strong enough to be weak." So, God *can* do anything that shows his strength, but he *can't* get rid of one of his attributes by failing in some area.

God cannot do things that are the opposite of truth (like breaking the law of non-contradiction), and he cannot be weak.

God can do everything that is logically possible, and he can do everything that is good, but he cannot do what is bad, and he cannot break the law of non-contradiction because that idea doesn't even make any sense. *In fact, if you could break the law of non-contradiction, then that means you could also not break it at the same time!*

Now, it is interesting to note that, though the vast majority of thinkers in church history believed that God could not break the law of non-contradiction, there have been some who thought that he could. Martin Luther and René Descartes thought that God could do the logically impossible. St. Augustine didn't think God could do the impossible, but he did think that God could count to infinity (which may be a logical impossibility). So, the issue is not completely solved. But, for the most part, people have believed that God cannot break the law of non-contradiction—not just that he *will not* but that he *cannot*.

So now we are ready to address two questions regarding logic and God. First, can God make a rock so big he cannot move it? Second, does the doctrine of the Trinity break the law of non-contradiction?

The trick to answering the first question is to realize that it is not a real question; it is a trick question—a linguistic wolf in question's clothing. The question really asks, "Is God strong enough to not be strong?" or "Can one of God's strengths contradict another one of God's strengths?" *The question itself makes no sense because the question contains a contradiction.* The question asks, "Can God destroy his strength with his own strength?" We don't have to answer this question for the same reason that we didn't have to answer whether the sentence "This sentence is false" was true earlier. It is a contradiction.

25

So that's the answer to that question. Go ahead, impress your friends!

Now on to the next question: Is the doctrine of the Trinity a logical contradiction? The short answer is no. The Trinity is logically consistent and is not a contradiction. But let's see why.

The historic, orthodox, biblical understanding of the Trinity is that there is only one God who eternally exists as three distinct persons, each of whom is fully God. To say it a simpler way, God is one in being and three in person at the same time.

You can see why the Trinity is not a contradiction. We are not saying that God is one being and God is not one being. That would be a contradiction. We are not saying that God is three persons and God is not three persons. That would be a contradiction. We are saying that God is one *being,* and God is three *persons.* We have not committed a contradiction because the words *being* and *person* mean different things. There is one and only one God— there is only one thing in the universe that is God, but there subsists within the divine essence three distinct persons who are each fully God at the same time. We have good definitions in church history of what we mean by *being* and *person*, but as long as those words don't mean the exact same thing, then we have not committed a contradiction.

Is this a mystery? Yes. Can you fully grasp God's Trinitarian nature? No way. Is it a paradox that we can learn more about but never fully comprehend? Yes. But is it a contradiction? It is not.

Equal Truths

Before we end this chapter, we must discuss one more thing that often throws people for a loop. Christians hold that the Bible is true, but is it *more* true than a truth found outside the Bible?

Which of the following sentences is *more* true?

"Two plus two equals four."

"Jesus died for our sins."

Answer: *They are equally true.* One of these truths is from mathematics, and one is from the Bible, but they are both equally true. All truths are equally true. By this I don't mean the idea that everyone has their own truth (that was refuted in the chapter on absolute truth). Rather, I mean that *if something is objectively true, then it is just as objectively true as another objectively true thing.*

How about these sentences—which of these is *more* true?

"Humans are mammals."

"A part cannot be larger than the whole."

"God is kind."

Again, they are all equally true. The first is a true claim from science. The second is a true claim from philosophy. The third is a true claim from the Bible.

To clarify, *even though all truths are equally true, some truths are more important than others.* The truths contained in the Bible are what God requires you to know, believe, and practice. The sentence "The Earth has one moon" and the sentence "Jesus was raised from the dead" are both true, but you are not required to know anything about the moon for salvation. In theology, when we ascribe to what is called the "sufficiency of scripture," this does not mean we believe there are no truths outside the Bible; *it means that the Bible (and the Bible alone) contains all that God requires you to know and do.* It is the ultimate standard that critiques other standards and is critiqued by none. There are truths in history and science. There are truths in philosophy and math. But the Bible alone is what God requires you to know.

I say this so we are not tempted to think that other fields of inquiry are bad. We are free to use whatever is true in our thinking. All truth is God's truth. This is especially true when it comes to philosophy. We are not allowed to get rid of all the good, rigorous, true thinking done by philosophers just because "that's philosophy, and it's not from the Bible."[1]

If all truths are equally true and we are allowed to use thinking outside the Bible as long as it's true, what special part does the Bible play in our thinking when it comes to logic? I can think of three things:

1. The Bible is often clearer than the ideas in other fields.
2. The Bible is what God actually requires you to know and believe.
3. The Bible is not mixed with error.

It's not that a claim in the Bible is more true than another claim. Rather, it's that the claims in the Bible are perfect, more important (because the Bible tells you who God is and how to be saved), and often easier to understand. The Bible stands over all. It is, in the Protestant tradition, the *norma norman non normata*—the "norm of norms, which is not normed." It is the thing by which we judge everything else and is, itself, judged by nothing. But that doesn't mean we ignore philosophy, tradition, creeds, councils, or church history.

Right now, it seems like science and Christianity are at odds with each other. That is not because they actually are at odds. They just seem to be at odds because we don't know everything about science, and we don't know everything about the Bible. If we did, there would be no conflict. You see, God knows everything there is to know about science, and God knows everything there is to know about the Bible, and there is no conflict in his mind. The only reason we think these things are at odds with each other is because we are not perfect theologians, and we are not perfect scientists. We don't know everything about theology, and we don't know everything about science.

So, feel free to study science, philosophy, history, and any other field of inquiry. But know that if any of those fields conflict with the Bible and you are interpreting the Bible correctly, you must realize that there has been an error in your thinking somewhere along the way. The error is never with the Bible. The error is with something said in one of those other fields.

CHAPTER 5

language

The concept of language is absolutely amazing when you stop and think about it. I can get you to think about something simply by opening a hole in my face (that I use to eat food) and making some articulate grunts. And it's not just that my language can describe things. The philosopher J. L. Austin showed how we can make things happen with our words. We can use what is called "performative language." When I'm performing a wedding and I say, "I now pronounce you husband and wife," I'm not describing that they are husband and wife. I'm not merely saying, "I see that you two are already married." I'm actually making it happen. Just by my proclamation they move from not being married to being married. That is amazing. Or when a judge sentences someone as guilty, the judge, by a mere utterance, has changed that person's life forever. When we christen a ship, tell a lie, break a promise, curse, bless, or yell "bomb" on an airplane, we are not merely using words to describe something. We are using words to impact life.

But this is just one way we can use words. With words we can ask questions, order food, describe events, flirt, give commands, and a million other things. It is crazy how many things we can do by simply stringing sounds together. Language is like an unruly animal that we can never quite tame. Bertrand Russell and Ludwig Wittgenstein, some of the greatest analytical philosophers of all time, tried to turn all language into logic and make it as precise as a logical syllogism only to find out that it couldn't be done perfectly.

Why are we talking about language in a book about logic? Well, because logical propositions are stated using language, so we have to say something about it. There are so many ways we can go wrong with our thinking. We don't have time to fully get into an entire "philosophy of language" here, but it is helpful to mention some things about language to clarify our thinking as it relates to logic.

For example, consider this sentence:

"Pegasus has wings."

Remember that logic deals with propositions, and this is, indeed, a proposition. Also notice that propositions are either true or false. But is this sentence true or false? Well, you may be tempted to say that it is true because, in Greek mythology, Pegasus does have wings. *However, how can the sentence be true if Pegasus does not exist?* How can any fact be true about a non-existing entity? Notice that the question is not, "Do people think that, according to Greek mythology, Bellerophon's steed has wings?" The sentence is simply, "Pegasus has wings."

Is the sentence "Santa has reindeer" true if (spoiler alert) Santa doesn't exist? You would not say, "Well, in the kid's stories about

Santa, he has reindeer, so the sentence, 'Santa has reindeer,' is true in reality." You see, even in something as simple as talking about Pegasus or Santa, we run into the puzzle of how to talk about non-existing things. Language is really tricky. Additionally, this puzzle shows us how language often implies things that it does not say explicitly. The sentence "Pegasus has wings" assumes that Pegasus (and even wings) exists, which it does not say explicitly but only by implication.

If that wasn't hard enough, the use of definitions complicates things further. A definition is meant to give you a description of something. It is meant to put something into a particular category. According to a famous story, which may be just a legend, Socrates defined a human as a "featherless biped." The story has it that a man in the audience, after hearing this definition, went home, plucked a chicken, brought it back, and threw it at Socrates's feet, saying, "Behold your human!"

When you define something, you need a definition that relates it to some category that other people already know (a similarity), but it also must show the difference or uniqueness of the thing being defined. You need to give a similarity and a difference. Let's say that someone wants a definition of the word *murder*. You cannot say that "murder is anytime someone dies," because that definition is too broad. People die from crocodile attacks, shark attacks, and lion attacks, but those are not considered to be murder (unless they are being used by a Bond villain). So, you might try to further refine the definition and say that "murder is anytime someone is killed by someone else." But that is not right either. Killing in self-defense or in war or to protect a village from a genocidal dictator is not murder—even though killing takes place. So, you might try something more precise and say that "murder is only when someone unjustly kills another person by stabbing them." But now you've made the definition too narrow. Surely, murder can be committed in ways other than stabbing. So, we have to try again; we may define murder as "an act whereby someone unjustly takes the life of another." You can't have your definition be too broad (e.g., all killing is murder), but it also cannot be too specific (e.g., murder is only if you poison someone).

Emotion in Language

We are emotional creatures. Emotion is not bad; it is just deceiving. Logic is always true, but emotions often lie to us. Language and rhetoric are notorious for using the emotional component of language to try to overshadow logical relations.

Consider the following two sentences:

> "To lower your blood pressure, I would recommend losing a few pounds."

> "Why don't you try getting on a treadmill, fatty."

Here is what is interesting about this example: Both sentences are telling a person to lose weight. However, the first sentence is much kinder and may be said by a doctor. The second sentence is really mean and may be said by some narcissistic jerk in the gym. Consider the emotional connection that comes with the second sentence. What is so crazy is that the content of the two sentences is pretty much the same, but the emotional baggage in the second sentence makes it seem like it is different (in all ways) from the first.

Or envision the difference between these two questions:

> "Do you love your child enough to spank them?"

> "Do you hit your child?"

Someone who is for corporal punishment would use the first sentence. And someone who is against spanking would use the second one. Notice how sly and seductive language can be. Language carries emotional baggage with it, and the job of the logician is to be able to cut through all the fluff and figure out what is really being said.

Consider these terms:

Racist
Fascist
Violent speech
Safe space
Healthcare
Rights
Sexist
Bigot
Hate

Think about how these terms are used in our culture. They are often used, not to make legitimate arguments, but as *linguistic Trojan horses*. They are used to ignore logic and sneak in cultural bias.

This leads to the difference between connotation and denotation. Denotation is the actual thing to which you are referring. Connotation is the baggage that comes with it. If I tell my wife that she looks skinny, that is not the same as if I say she looks slender. The denotation of both words is pretty similar; they both state that my wife is not overweight. But *skinny* makes it sound like she is too thin and sickly, whereas *slender* sounds more beautiful and elegant.

Determining Meaning

Who or what determines the meaning of a word? You may be tempted to say, "a dictionary." But that just pushes the question back one step further; how does the dictionary editor know what words mean? Webster, whoever he is, is not God. He does not get to determine what words mean. What do you do when two dictionaries disagree or when a dictionary lists several definitions for the word you are trying to understand? We use some words for years before they are ever added to a dictionary.

That is not how dictionaries work. Dictionaries don't get to determine what words mean; *they tell you how a culture is already using a word.* Dictionaries don't prescribe; they *describe* how a word is already used in a particular setting. That is why you have new words added to the dictionary every now and again. As a word is used by a particular group of people at a particular time, a dictionary tries to represent how that word is used in that society.

A dictionary (or "lexicon" if you are a language student) only *gives you a range of possible meanings.* For example, let's take the word *run.* What does *run* mean? You might say that the word *run* refers to what we do when we are going faster than walking. But doesn't the word also have many other meanings? With just a simple Google search, I found that *run* can mean several things: You can run (verb). You can participate in a 5K fun run (noun). You can run for office. Your nose can run. A bus or boat may have a particular repeated journey that it takes called a run. You can run a corporation as a boss. Your refrigerator can run (hence the prank-call joke). A woman can have a run in her hose. You can even smuggle narcotics and be called a drug *run*ner. So, let's say I come across a sentence that says:

> "As the criminal sprinted away from the cops, he caused them to run after him."

If I look in a dictionary, I may be given 12 different uses of the word *run.* How do I know which one is right? Well, here is the big point I want you to take away: *Words get their specific meaning from the context in which they occur. It is the context that determines the meaning of a word (within its historical and grammatical setting) as it is placed there intentionally by an author.* Context is king.

In the sentence above, I know that the word *run* refers to the physical act of running because of the context. The word *sprinted*, the word *away*, the phrase *after him*, and the fact that I have seen a lot of criminals run from the police in old episodes of *Cops* are all contextual indicators for what the word means in that sentence.

Words change their meaning (even in very slight ways) depending on the context.

Bottom Line: Pay attention to context when trying to understand a word in a particular instance. Most logical mistakes come from misdefining a word (more on this under "Equivocation" in "Part II – Logical Fallacies").

Language and God

Imagine that you are at a park on a beautiful spring day. You and some friends are having a picnic, and you see a squirrel on the trunk of a tree near you. You, being the spry athlete you are, decide that you are going to try to catch it. So, you start creeping up toward the squirrel. The only problem is that you can't sneak up on it very well because the squirrel always turns so that it can see you. So though you keep circling the tree, trying to get behind the squirrel, you never see the back of the squirrel because he always turns to keep you in view.

Here is the question: Have you gone *around* the squirrel?

William James, one of the great American intellectuals of the 1800s, tells a story about a debate he had with his friends regarding this very scenario. Some of them said that they did truly go around the squirrel (because they circled the tree), and others said that they did not go around the squirrel (because they only ever saw the squirrel's face—not his back).

What's the answer? Well, it all depends on what you mean by the word *around*. If you mean, "Did you circumnavigate the squirrel by going around the entire tree, including the squirrel?" the answer is yes. If you mean, "Did you ever get behind the squirrel and go around his back?" the answer is no.

Language can be tricky. Here we see what is called an equivocation, which occurs when you use the same word (in this case, the word *around*) in two different ways.

What does this strange squirrel example have to do with talking about God?[1]

Just stick with me as I explain. There are basically three ways to use words when comparing two things:

> **Equivocally:** When the word that is used can be interpreted in two or more different ways. Equivocal language is what we see in the squirrel example above. There is debate about whether one has gone around the squirrel because the word *around* is being used in two different ways.

> **Analogically:** When one word is used to have a similar or analogous meaning as another. Analogical language is when two things can be compared, but not perfectly—it is just an analogy. Everything doesn't literally hold true of two things that are compared. If I say that a powerful football player is like "an ox," I don't mean that he literally has horns, four legs, and isn't human. What I mean is that he

is strong. A strong human and an ox are not exactly the same, but you get the point of what I'm saying: The football player is *really* strong.

Univocally: When one word is used to have exactly the same meaning as another. Univocal language is when you use a word that has exactly the same meaning when comparing two things. If I say, "Albert Einstein was smart," and I say, "Jonathan Edwards was smart," I'm meaning the same thing by the word *smart.* They were both two really intelligent humans. When it comes to human intelligence, one may be smarter than the other (I'd take Edwards over Einstein in an intellectual cage match), but the word I'm using to draw the comparison (i.e., *smart*) doesn't change its meaning qualitatively.

So, here is the million-dollar question:

When the Bible says that God has a "mighty right arm" or he "remembers his covenant" or he gathers us under the shadow of his "wings" or he speaks with Moses "face-to-face" or he "changes his mind," are these things to be taken equivocally, analogically, or univocally?

Let's take the sentence "God is love."

When we say that "God is love," we can't say that the word *love* should be used in an equivocal sense. If we do, then we can also say that the Bible teaches that "God is a score of zero in tennis" (which is also called "love"). But that's not what the Bible means. We can't say the word *love* has nothing to do with literal love. If all language about God is equivocal, then we can't know anything about God! So it appears that equivocation, when used about God, gets us into the same trouble of William James and the squirrel.

On the other end of the spectrum is the view of one of the most influential Christian thinkers of the Middle Ages: John Duns Scotus. In fact, Scotus was so brilliant and his arguments so technical that his students had trouble reproducing his thoughts accurately. For their misunderstanding, they were called "dunces" (named after John Duns Scotus), which is where we get the idea of people wearing cone-shaped hats (with the word *dunce* on them) as a punishment for saying something dumb in class. Scotus held to a doctrine of univocity whereby our language about God must, in some sense, mean the same thing that it means when it is used by us. So, if we say that "God is an infinite being" and "a cow is a finite being," we are not saying that God's essence is the same thing as a cow's essence. Rather, we are saying that our concept of "being" has to be the same for both or else how could we ever know anything about God at all? Now, that sounds kind of nerdy and technical, and we don't have time to get into Scotus's defense of this view.

Though Scotus was extremely smart, God's nature is so different from ours that Scotus's view runs into some problems. For example, when I say that "God is loving" and I say that "my dog is loving," univocal language makes the word *loving* too close in meaning between the two sentences, which distorts my view of God and makes the Creator too much like creation. Scotus's view might run into intellectual idolatry (though defenders of Scotus will deny this).

Enter the most influential Christian thinker in the Middle Ages: St. Thomas from a town in Italy called Aquino—he is better known as Thomas Aquinas. One of his major contributions to theology was to defend the idea that when language is used about God, it is used analogically. This is the position that I think is correct. When we say that "God is love," we don't mean that we have no idea of what love means (equivocation). We also don't mean that it is the same concept of love that I have (univocation). Instead, we can use the fact that we love people to give us an analogy of what God's love must be like, but his love is on a totally different spectrum than ours. God is love, yes, but love means something qualitatively different when used to identify an infinite being than when it is used of finite beings. The sentence "God is love" is absolutely true: Aquinas would say it is even literally true, but it doesn't mean that "God is love just like you and I understand the word *love*." God is loving, but love means something very different to God than it means to us.

Perhaps an analogy would be helpful at this point. If my car was running low on gas, I might say that "my car is getting thirsty." Of course, you know what I mean even though my car is not literally thirsty. I mean something like this: "My car needs liquid, and I'm using an analogy of times when I need liquid, though a car is never literally thirsty because it is a different kind of entity than I am."

It is important to remember that God is completely "other." He is completely unlike everything that is created. He does not have a body because he is Spirit (John 4:24), he is not bound by time because he is eternal (Ps. 90:2), he is not bound by space because he is omnipresent (Jer. 23:23–24; 1 Kings 8:26), he doesn't need anything because he possesses aseity[2] (Acts 17:24–25), you can't see God's essence because he is invisible (1 Tim. 1:17), he is unchanging (James 1:17; Mal. 3:6), and he knows everything (1 John 3:20). In addition to that, he is one, simple substance and is not composite or composed of parts. God is a Trinity—one God who consists of three distinct persons who are each fully God but distinct from each other—all at the same time. God is being;

he is not becoming. He is pure actuality with no potentiality. Whatever he is he is that thing all the way, all the time.

Chapter II of the Westminster Confession of Faith says:

> There is but one only living and true [Triune] God, who is infinite in being and perfection, a most pure spirit, invisible, without body, parts, or passions; immutable, immense, eternal, incomprehensible, almighty, most wise, most holy, most free, most absolute, working all things according to the counsel of His own immutable and most righteous will, for His own glory; most loving, gracious, merciful, long-suffering, abundant in goodness and truth, forgiving iniquity, transgression, and sin, the rewarder of them that diligently seek Him; and withal, most just, and terrible in His judgments; hating all sin, and who will by no means clear the guilty.

In fact, God is so infinitely unlike creation that many theologians in the Middle Ages thought you could only describe God by what he is not. This is known as the *via remotionis, via negativa,* or, in Greek Orthodoxy, "apophatic theology." These fancy phrases simply promote the view that we can't say what God is. We can only say what he is not. So, when we say God is "infinite," we are really saying he is "not finite." When we say God is "loving," we are really saying he is "not unloving," etc.

But there are a few problems with trying to talk about God only in negatives:

1. The Bible talks about God in positive terms.
2. You cannot describe something using only negatives without assuming something positive. (For example, if

you don't know what a dog is and I say, "Well, it is not a lizard and it is not a cow and it is not a car," that doesn't tell you what a dog is).

3. In Christianity, the highest object of our love, as Scotus would say, is not a negative.

All these theologians and their big words are just trying to answer this question: How on earth do you talk about a being who is Trinity, non-composite, infinite, eternal, outside time and space, unchanging, all-knowing, and spiritual with language that we use as humans who are none of these things?

Well, the answer is the realization that all our language about God is *analogical.*

God is not a man, but the only language we have is human language. Our language is always constrained when we talk about God. We can know God truly, but we cannot know him fully. We can apprehend but not comprehend him. When God talks to us in scripture, he, according to Calvin, lisps to us as a mother does to her children.[3]

You see, God doesn't literally have a mighty right "hand." If he did, how big are his fingernails? Are they made up of dead skin cells? Does A+ blood run through the veins in his hand? Does he have fingerprints so he can better grip things? Do his hands get waterlogged when soaked in water? You see that all these questions are absolutely ridiculous. God doesn't look like a man just because the Bible says he has a "hand" any more than he looks like a bird just because the psalmist says he has "wings" or like a plant because he speaks to Moses through a "burning bush."

If you want to try to use this type of language literally, you run into a lot of problems. Now you have to say that God literally has wings. You have to say that God literally has seven eyes (Zech.

4:10). You have to say that God literally looks like a smoking fire pot (Gen. 15:17). You have to say that God literally forgets things. You have to say that God looks like a cow (after all, when the Hebrews at Sinai wanted to make an idol of God, they made a golden calf).

You see, when you read a phrase about God's mighty right hand, you are not supposed to take that in an equivocal sense and think the word "hand" means something like, "God has a full house in a game of poker," which would also be a "hand." Nor are you to take it in a univocal sense and act like the concept of God's "hand" is like yours. God doesn't have a hand or any body parts because he is infinite spiritual essence.

Rather, you are supposed to understand "hand" in an analogical way. Most people are right-handed, and their right hand is their "strong" hand, so you are supposed to know that God is strong too. Now, the difference between our strength and God's strength is not one of quantity; it is one of quality. It is not as though we are on the same scale, and he is just higher up on the scale. We are on two totally different scales when it comes to "strength."

The Bible demonstrates this in several places. Consider an example from 1 Samuel 15. It says that God regretted something, and also says that he does not regret things:

> The word of the LORD came to Samuel: "I regret that I have made Saul king, for he has turned back from following me and has not performed my commandments."
>
> —1 Samuel 15:10–11

> And also the Glory of Israel will not lie or have regret, for he is not a man, that he should have regret.
>
> —1 Samuel 15:29

44

Notice how language is used of God analogically. It says God "regrets," but then it goes on to say in effect that just in case you think God "really" regrets, you are mistaken; God is not a man, so *regret* means something different for him than for you. And the same is true regarding God "remembering" or "burning with anger" or anything that is said about God.

It is not just the case that some of the descriptions of God are constrained by human language, but all the language we use when we talk about God is constrained by human language. *It is not as though the Bible contains just a few anthropomorphisms (describing God in human terms though he is not human); the entire Bible is anthropomorphic when it talks about God.* We never think of God perfectly because we cannot think infinite thoughts.

So what? Why is this helpful to know?

I have found that many of our problems in life come down to thinking that God is like us. We think of him as a really big man on a cloud. We think that because humans' love for us varies depending on our behavior, God's must as well. We think that we give him good and bad days based on how we are acting. We assume that because humans break their promises, then God must do so as well. We assume that because humans have bad reasons for making laws, then God's rules must not be for our good. We assume that we are smarter than God in some areas and that we would do things differently than he does.

But that is idolatry.

If you are thinking of God in creaturely categories, you are committing mental idolatry.

It is not as though God is just all your attributes to a higher degree. He is qualitatively different. You live in a house; he inhabits eternity (Isa. 57:15). You are one human, one person. God is one God, three persons. You are created, changing, bodily, and limited. God is uncreated, unchanging, spirit, and unlimited. God is not a man (Num. 23:19).

"But what about Christ?" you may ask.

Even in the person of Christ, who is both God and man, his natures are not mixed (a heresy known as Eutychianism). Jesus's deity does not change just because he also has humanity. His two natures are distinct though Jesus is only one person. Even in the incarnation nothing changes about Christ's deity. He doesn't lay aside his "God-ness" or get rid of any of his divine attributes. He takes on a second nature (humanity), but nothing about his divine nature changes. Jesus is fully human, but this is a second nature, not a point where you should think of his deity as human.

This mystery should lead us to worship. It should cause us to bow down and repent of our pride and worship at the mystery of our infinite, Triune God. May we repent for making God in our image and for exalting humanity to the same level as God. May we realize that God's nature is mysterious and beyond our full comprehension. May knowing how different he is from us cause us to trust his infinite power more and more.

CHAPTER 6

presuppositions

I was talking about presuppositions one time and I asked for a volunteer. A young man came up onstage, and I said to him, "I want you to draw on the whiteboard only what I tell you to draw, no more and no less." He agreed to the challenge. I told him, "Okay, I want you to draw a picture of Humpty Dumpty sitting on a wall." The guy began to draw a picture of the character in the famous nursery rhyme. When he was finished, there was a picture of an egg that had a smiley face sitting on a brick wall.

The man thought he did a pretty good job of following my instructions until I asked this question:

"Why did you draw Humpty Dumpty as an egg?"

I didn't say he was an egg.

The nursery rhyme doesn't say he is an egg.

We just assume he is an egg before we even begin the story. That is a presupposition. It is something that you assume before you even begin an argument. Not to mention that the guy drew him with a smiley face (though I didn't say he had a smiley face in my sentence).

Think back to the children's song "Bingo." The first line says, "There was a farmer who had a dog and Bingo was his name-O." But whose name is "Bingo"? The farmer or the dog? It is most likely the dog, but it could be the famer as well, as in, "There was a farmer who had a dog, and the farmer's name was 'Bingo.'" The song never says that is the name of the dog nor is there any more information about the dog in the song.

We just assume it. That is a presupposition.

Imagine the following scenario. There are three people on a boat: the president, a three-year-old little girl, and a 90-year-old man who has cancer.

Now, for the sake of this illustration (and regardless of who is in office when you read this book), pick a president you like. I will pick Teddy Roosevelt because he was a hard-core tough guy who had a chest tattoo, and that's my kind of president.

So, a president (you like), a three-year-old little girl, and a 90-year-old man who has cancer are all on a boat, and they fall off. Now, for the sake of this illustration, they cannot swim, and you can only save one of them. Who do you save?

Before you pretend to be Jason Bourne and try to explain how you would use your tactical skills to save all of them, that is not the point of the exercise. We would all try to save all of them if we could. But you can only choose one. Whom do you choose and why?

Every time I have asked this question, I have gotten one of two answers:

Some people say, "the president," and when I ask why, they say, "because he has a really important job."

Other people say, "the little girl," and when I ask why, they say, "because she is so little—she has so much life left to live."

But you know who nobody ever chooses? The 90-year-old man. Why? Because he doesn't have much life left to live.

Because we are Americans and because we have been subtly influenced by pragmatism, we assume that his life is less valuable *because it is less productive.* We have forgotten that humans have inherent value. One's value does not depend on how productive they are or how long they have to live. But we don't even consider this. Someone who is 90 and has cancer doesn't have much life left to live. We conclude that the few years they do have left are somehow less valuable because there are fewer of them. We turn his humanity into a number and, since it is a low number, we are more comfortable with him dying than we are with the other characters.

This is what is known as a presupposition.

A presupposition is an assumption or a starting point that you bring into an argument. A presupposition is what you think before you think. It is something you suppose—"pre." It is something you assume beforehand at the beginning of an argument. We all have presuppositions. *You cannot get rid of presuppositions altogether. Instead, the best you can do is be aware of them, so you know where you are tempted to skew something in the direction of your worldview.* We cannot get rid of our assumptions, but we can be aware of what they are. We can be aware of what we *want* the truth to be, and we can even change our assumptions over time.

Here is another example:

I once heard a professor ask students to name some things that were in the classroom. The students began looking around the room and naming things they saw: chairs, tables, desks, chalkboard, pens, paper, books, etc.

The professor then said something to this effect:

> That's interesting. Most of you named individual, physical objects in the room. Some of you, who are clever, may have mentioned really specific things like pages in the books or words on a page, and some of you who are really smart might have named things like light and air . . .
>
> But, the professor continued, why didn't any of you name "existence"? That is certainly in the room too. Why didn't any of you name "beside"? That relationship is certainly in the room as well—notice that I am standing *beside* the podium. Why didn't any of you name "standing"? Why didn't any of you name numbers? Why didn't any of you name colors? My tie is red so "redness" must be in the room as well. There are quite a lot of things you didn't mention![1]

Why is it that the students only named individual, physical objects and not the more abstract things the professor mentioned? They did so because the students had assumptions that they had never stopped to think about.

The students were American and so, whether they knew it or not, they had been influenced by Aristotle. Aristotle taught that there were 10 categories of "being," but his primary one was individual things. A dog, a tree, a table, etc. were the most "real" things to Aristotle. That is why the students named individual objects in the room.

Now, did the students know that Aristotle's philosophy had influenced them? No. Had most of the students ever even read Aristotle? No. Yet, a philosophical movement had influenced them subtly just by the fact that they lived in America. It just happened to be the air they breathed.

To say it again: *You cannot get rid of presuppositions.* There is no such thing as not having any presuppositions. Even if you say, "I don't have any presuppositions," you have already presupposed several things:

> That you are speaking.
>
> That I can hear you.
>
> That your words have meaning.
>
> That words exist.
>
> That I am a human.
>
> That your position is not a contradiction.
>
> That not-having-presuppositions is possible.

And I could name many more!

So, if we never come to evidence totally unbiased and if we cannot get rid of our presuppositions, is there any hope of us being able to come to a correct view on an issue?

The answer is yes. But it's not because we can get rid of our presuppositions; *it is because we can be aware of our presuppositions, and we can know where our beginning assumptions might lead us astray.*

It's like we are all wearing different colored glasses. We cannot take off the glasses to see, in a completely unbiased way, all the colors of the objects around us. But what we can do is learn about the color of the glasses that we are wearing. We can ask others what color lenses their glasses have, and we can see how other people in history have thought about issues by studying their glasses.

For example, if I'm wearing green-tinted glasses and someone shows me a white piece of paper, I will be tempted to say that it is green. But if I know that my glasses are green-tinted, I will pause and think to myself, "Everything looks green to me because of my presuppositions, but since I know my glasses are biased, the paper may actually be a color other than green."

When a Christian and an atheist get together to debate, they often pretend like they don't have any presuppositions. The Christian agrees that he will put his beliefs aside (temporarily) and just argue "logically." The atheist agrees that he will put his disbelief aside (temporarily) and just argue "logically." Both of them act like they can really get rid of the deepest truths they hold and then somehow step onto some morally neutral, assumption-free mental octagon to fight it out.

But that is impossible.

If Christianity is true, you cannot pretend like it isn't. If atheism is true, then why on earth would it be rational to pretend like it's not? *How will either side prove truth while (pretending) to step away from it?* It would be better for the Christian to just admit that he thinks Christianity is true and that he cannot pretend like it isn't. It would be better for the atheist to just admit that he thinks atheism is true and that he cannot pretend like it isn't. Let's not act as though we don't have presuppositions; *let's acknowledge our presuppositions and then see whose are most logical.*

Everyone has presuppositions, but that doesn't mean everyone's presuppositions are equal. Some presuppositions are much better than others. Let's lay out what Christians believe and lay out what atheists believe and really look at them. Both systems have "holes" in them—both systems have problems that they cannot answer. But which system has fewer holes? Which system has better presuppositions? Neither worldview is bulletproof (at least not from the perspective of limited humanity), but perhaps one worldview is more consistent and makes more sense of the data than the other.

Whether it is in theology, politics, ethics, or anything else, we have to be aware of our presuppositions and the presuppositions of our culture.

This is especially true in studying argumentation. When we come to an argument, we bring a million presuppositions to the table. Are we aware of them? Are we aware of how we want to skew the information so that we can affirm the position we already hold? Are we willing to allow others to correct us even though it means admitting that we are wrong? Are we willing to change a political position or a theological position if a good enough case can be made? Or are we merely wanting to stay where we are no matter what evidence is presented? What position do we *hope* is true, and how might that bias our thinking? What position do we *want* to be true?

There are times I'm discussing an issue with someone and they seem to be unwilling to change their mind no matter where the discussion goes and no matter what evidence I present. I sometimes stop and ask, "What evidence could be presented to you that would cause you to change your mind, or is your mind already made up so that no matter what evidence I give, you will not change?" Even if you are dead set on a position, you should at least know what evidence *could* change your mind *if* it could be presented. If no evidence could change your mind on a topic, then you have ceased to act like a rational human being and have resorted to personal, arrogant, dogmatism. You've probably seen that a lot in our culture. People don't really repent anymore; they just double down and dig their heels in even after being shown that they were wrong.

Many of us, myself included, make mistakes in reasoning because we are not aware of the assumptions we bring into an argument. If we were more aware of our presuppositions, we wouldn't make as many mistakes in our thinking.

Envision that you are going to a work-related party and your boss comes up and says to you, "What are you doing here?" If you think that your boss doesn't like you, you will assume he meant this comment negatively. If you think your boss likes you, you will assume this is a friendly question and that the boss is happy you came.

The sentence didn't change. It is the exact same sentence in both scenarios. But your presuppositions may have made you hear it in a way that your boss didn't intend. Just because people have different presuppositions doesn't mean that there is not absolute truth or a right answer. Absolute truth exists in reality. False presuppositions, though, obscure your ability to see that objective truth for yourself.

Everything comes down to presuppositions. This is the central reason people disagree and why so many people argue past each other. To be a good logician, you are going to have to be aware of your presuppositions and the presuppositions of your opponents. You can't get rid of presuppositions. And you don't need to. Presuppositions can be good. When I assume that if I walk into traffic, I will get hurt, I'm holding to a good and helpful presupposition. When I assume that the sun will rise tomorrow and, therefore, make plans accordingly, that is a good presupposition. *The goal is to try to make your assumptions explicit* although they are most often very hidden and lie below the surface.

I once had a New Testament professor ask me a question that I thought was very interesting. He said, "Zach, no matter how much research you did, would you ever come to the conclusion that Jesus is *not* God?" I said, "No . . . because he is God." He said, "You see, you ended up where you began. You began thinking Jesus was God, and you ended thinking Jesus was God. That is what a presupposition is. And the same is true for someone who didn't believe Jesus was God. No matter how much research they did, they would probably end up not thinking he was God; they would end up where they began as well."

That is a presupposition. With a presupposition, your starting point will determine your end point. If your starting point is logical and true, your conclusion will be sound. But if your starting point is wrong, everything else will be wrong.

Worldview

One of the phrases that most annoys me is when someone says that they are "not religious" or that they "don't have a religion." Now, I totally understand what they are saying. They mean to say that they are an atheist or an agnostic but just don't want to use those terms because they sound mean. So far, so good. But the concept of "religion" can be confusing. So, let me pose the issue a different way. Whether or not everyone has a religion, everyone does have a *worldview*. A worldview is . . . drumroll . . . a way of viewing the world. Everyone has a view about God, even if their view is that he doesn't exist. Everyone has a belief about morality, even if they believe that morality is relative. Everyone has a view of what happens to them after they die, even if they think that we just become worm food. In short, everyone has a worldview.

When someone says they are nonreligious, they are acting as though they are neutral. But most don't realize that *they must prove their worldview as well*. To say it stronger, there is no neutral worldview. Everyone has things they believe that have to be based on evidence. If you are nonreligious, you are a secularist, and you have to give an answer to life's deepest questions as well.

Additionally, one has to be *consistent with their worldview.* If you believe, for example, that morality is just based on societal opinion—what a society says is good or bad—then you have to hold that if a society says assaulting children is okay, then it may be okay for them. If you don't think assaulting children is okay, then you will have to change what you think it is that makes something moral. If mankind is merely an evolved ape and the purpose of life is just to promote your offspring, then it makes no sense for you to refrain from killing a man and sleeping with his wife if you can get away with it. You just can't play both sides. You always have to be consistent no matter what worldview you hold.

Don't get me wrong; I know that there are humanitarian answers to the issues above. What I am trying to point out is how inconsistent most of us are in our worldviews. I once had a friend who was a Muslim woman who believed that homosexuality was okay. She didn't realize the inconsistency in her worldview. Islam condemns homosexuality. So, she either has to say that Islam is wrong on this point or that homosexuality is wrong on this point, but they are not both right at the same time. All of us must be consistent with our worldviews regardless of our religious or nonreligious backgrounds.

CHAPTER 7

deductive versus inductive arguments

L et's talk about two kinds of arguments that are easy to accidentally mix up. These two types are deductive arguments and inductive arguments.

We will look at them in reverse order. What is an inductive argument? Induction means that you look at several, individual cases and then make a general, grand conclusion.

For example, if I find that water boils at 212°F (100°C, for my British friends), then I have merely performed one experiment.[1] If I try boiling water a second time, it also boils at 212°F. If I then try 248 more times, water always seems to boil at 212°F. Based on what I have seen, I would then conclude, "Water always boils at 212°F."

Notice some really important things about induction:

1. It involves experience.
2. It reaches beyond looking at a proposition and looks at the actual world.
3. It is bottom-up; meaning, you look at individual things and then create a larger theory. It moves from particulars to universals.
4. It's practical knowledge.
5. *Induction only allows you to state things with probability and never certainty.*

Let's look at this last claim in a little more detail. Just because water has always boiled at 212°F up until now, *I have absolutely no reason to think that this could not change in the future.* Now, don't get me wrong, I don't think water-boiling temperatures are going anywhere—I'm not some crazy water-temperature conspiracy theorist. But *I cannot prove that it's impossible for them to change.* Notice there is nothing inherently contradictory about water changing properties in the future to boil at 213°F. In fact, at a different altitude the boiling point does indeed change. There is nothing logically contradictory about thinking of a world that God could have made in which water boiled at a different temperature.

Let me give you a clearer example if that last paragraph was a bit confusing:

Let's say I see one crow that is black. I then see another crow that is black. I then see 248 more crows that are black. I might make the statement "All crows are black." However, this statement is not certain. It is only probable. I haven't looked at all the crows that have ever existed. I could be wrong. It turns out that this particular statement is indeed wrong. There are albino crows (they look terrifying, by the way). You see, my inductive statement is not logically certain. It is only probable. Evidence could come up later that would contradict what my theory has been up until that point. No matter how many times I add two plus two, it will always equal four, and it will do so with certainty. Induction, however, is not like that. An inductive statement can change depending on the data.

We have never found any unicorns in real life, but that only means that there is a very high probability that they do not exist. I have not looked everywhere in the universe and, therefore, I cannot say (with mathematical certainty) that there are no unicorns. I cannot prove that it is logically impossible that unicorns exist! To say it another way, God could have made a world with unicorns. Again, don't get me wrong. *I don't believe in unicorns* (or aliens or ghosts or the Loch Ness Monster or gum that never loses its flavor). But the reason I don't believe in them is because they are not likely, not because there is something in the very idea of them that contains a logical contradiction.

Now, deduction is the opposite of induction. Let's look at a deductive sentence:

"All bachelors are unmarried."

Notice that this sentence is very unlike the inductive ones above.

1. First, it is absolutely certain. If you know what a "bachelor" is and you know what the word *unmarried* means, then you realize that this sentence is, not only true, it cannot be false.

2. Second, notice that you don't have to do any experiments to prove it. Unlike the water-boiling, crow-counting, or

unicorn-searching above, it would not do you any good to go up to true bachelors and ask them if they are un-married.

3. There is no new information in the first part of the sentence that is not contained in the second part of the sentence. You know whether the sentence is true or false just by looking at the sentence itself.
4. The knowledge is more theoretical than practical.
5. Deduction involves what is top-down; the general (absolute) truth is then applied to all the particulars. It moves from universals down to individual cases.

Did you get all that?

To say it another way, induction is like science. It does experiments and then takes the finding of those experiments and makes probable (but never logically certain) conclusions. We know this because science changes all the time when a better (i.e., more probable) theory comes down the pike. For example, scientists used to think that to get rid of a fever, you should cut someone and let them bleed out all the bad, hot blood. We don't think that anymore (and that bloodletting is what killed George Washington).

Deduction is like math. It takes something on one side of the equal sign and shows how it matches the other side of the equal sign. If induction found results that were logically certain, then there would be no need to do experiments. Logical certainty is true whether it can be done once or an infinite number of times.

Can you tell which of the following sentences are deductive and which are inductive?

- The most common blood type in the world is O positive.
- All triangles have three sides.

- I exist.
- The earth has a core made up of magma.
- All rabbits are mammals.[2]

Now, there is some confusion that can arise if we forget that these are two very different types of inquiries. We should not treat inductive statements as if they are certain nor treat deductive statements as if they are not. We should realize that deductive statements don't give us as much practical information as inductive statements. We should realize that some sentences can be seen to be true or false just by looking at the sentence, and others can only be demonstrated by going out and observing the world.

For more about induction and deduction, check out "Confusing Probability and Possibility" in "Part II – Logical Fallacies."

CHAPTER 8

logic and syllogisms

This chapter contains a lot of the "meat and potatoes" of logic. I have tried to make this section as easy to understand and as simple as possible. Most textbooks make these things really complicated, and there is certainly a time for that. But since I have realized that every classmate that I have ever taken a logic class with forgets all the info in about six months anyway, I wanted to give you things that I hope will "stick."[1] You may need to read this slowly because it is a little more technical than the previous chapters.

Subject, Predicate, and Copula

Consider the sentence "John is a baseball player."

This sentence has a subject, a predicate, and a copula. A subject is the main topic addressed in the statement. In this case, it is "John." A subject is what is modified by the predicate. The predicate is simply the rest of the sentence. A predicate "says "something" about the subject. In this case "is a baseball player" is the predicate. It is what is "predicated" (i.e., "said") about the subject. The copula is some form of the word "to be" (in this case, "is") that links the subject with the rest of the statement.

Notice that there are two categories that are being compared here. The category of "John" and the category of "baseball players." This proposition is stating that the category of this one particular guy named "John" fits into the larger category of baseball players.

Now, pay attention to this part: *Every statement we deal with in logic can be turned into a statement that basically relates one category to another category.*

Consider the sentence "All eagles are birds."

The subject term is *eagles.*
The copula is *are.*
The predicate term is *birds.*

This statement is saying that the category of eagles fits into the larger category of birds.

In logic, we are always concerned with how two (or more) categories relate to each other. If we say, "All eagles are birds," we are comparing two categories and saying that one category (eagles) fits into the other category (birds). If we say, "Hot dogs are made of horse meat," we are comparing how the category of one thing (hot dogs) fits within the category of another (horse meat). If we say, "Some people are nice," we are fitting only some of those who fit into the category of people into the second category of nice things. If we say, "No dogs are human," we are saying that the category of dogs does not fit into the category of humans at all.

One really helpful way to see how two categories relate is to draw circles. You can use a Venn diagram or literally just draw one circle inside of another. Most of the technical aspects of logic come down to this simple idea: *We want to correctly understand how two categories relate to each other.* It's that simple! How does one circle (a category of things) fit within another circle (a different category of things).

Four Vowels to Remember (A, E, I, O)

There are four ways to deal with the quantity (some, all, none) and affirmation/negation of a statement. These are called "categorical propositions." Historically, they are assigned to vowels. (The vowels are based on Latin words, not English words, so don't let trying to understand why a particular letter is what it is trip you up). Universal means "all," particular means "some," affirmation means "is/are," and negation means "is/are not."

> A: Universal affirmation: "All cats are good."
> E: Universal negation: "No cats are good."
> I: Particular affirmation: "Some cats are good."
> O: Particular negation: "Some cats are not good."

It is important to realize how each of these sentences works for the sake of argumentation. Let's take an "A" type proposition (a "universal affirmation"):

> "All men are chauvinists."

Notice that this statement is claiming that every single man fits into the category of things that are chauvinists. If I drew circles to illustrate this proposition, I would have a big circle titled "chauvinists," and I would draw a little circle completely inside of it titled "men." Now, if someone made this claim and wanted other people to agree with them, notice how high the burden of proof is. *Making a universal claim obligates you to make sure there is not a single exception to that claim.* This claim says that there is not one man in history who was not a chauvinist. But, to show that this claim is false, I don't have to prove that "all men are not chauvinists." I don't have to give a universal in the other direction. To disprove a universal statement, I don't have to show that the opposite universal is true. Rather, I only have to show that there is just one example of a man in history who was not a chauvinist. So, here is a helpful debate tip: If someone makes a universal claim (all, no, every, etc.), you only need one counter example to debunk their entire claim. If someone says that "all men are chauvinists," all I have to do to defeat their entire (universal) claim is to tell them about my buddy Ted who is not chauvinistic at all.[2]

Also, notice that a particular affirmation (I) is assumed by a universal affirmation (A). If it is true that "all mammals have hearts," then the phrase "Some mammals have hearts" is true by default.

Also, notice that, if A = B is true, then B = A is true. Most of this is just common sense, but it is helpful to say it explicitly.

One more thing before we move on to the other vowels. Notice that something that is in its own category is, by default, a universal statement. What do I mean by that? Well, if I said, "Michael Jordan was a famous basketball player for the Chicago Bulls," notice that there is only one person who fits into the category "Michael Jordan." There might be other people with that same name, but there is only one Michael Jordan (who was the famous basketball star who also acted in the movie *Space Jam*). This is actually a universal claim: "All people who are the Michael Jordan (and there is only one) are those who are a famous basketball player for the Chicago Bulls." So, if a category only has one thing in it, then to mention that one thing is actually a universal statement.

Let's look at statements that produce universal negation. Suppose I give an "E" statement such as "No cats are good." If it can be shown that even one cat is good, then my statement is false. Thankfully, since cats are the worst, my claim is true!

If "no cats are good," then it is true that "some cats are not good." Again, a universal claim includes a particular claim (in this case an "E" statement contains an "O" statement by default).

If I make an "I" proposition, "Some people are kind," how many people do I have to show are kind before my claim is right? Answer: only one. *It is much easier to prove a particular affirmation than it is to prove a universal affirmation.* How do I disprove an "I" statement? Well, you might be tempted to say that I negate an "I" statement (a particular affirmation) with an "O" statement (a particular negation). But this is not correct. If I say that "some people are kind" (I) and you say, "No, actually, some people are not kind," (O) you have not refuted my claim because we can both be right. Some people can be kind, and some (other) people cannot be kind *at the same time.* This is the case in reality; some people are great, and some are the worst.

To show that a particular affirmation (I) is false, you have to negate it with a universal negation (E). If you want to show that my phrase "Some people are kind" is false, you have to show that "no people are kind."

The same is true with a particular negation. If I say, "Some people are not kind" (O), then the refutation of that claim has to be "All people are kind" (A).

The Syllogism

So, let's put all this together and make an actual argument. Notice that a proposition is not usually a full-blown argument. It can be a full-blown argument (two plus two is four is both an argument and a proposition). But typically, it requires more than just one statement. A proposition is just a sentence that claims something. If I say, "Stealing is a sin," that is just a claim. If I say, "Stealing is sin because the Bible says so," now I've begun to give reasons to support my claim. An argument gives additional propositions that bolster and support your claim.

Arguments can be laid out in their most basic parts by using what is called an Aristotelian Syllogism or a syllogism for short.

There are several ways to write them but here is a common example of a syllogism:

$A = B$
$B = C$
_____

Therefore, $A = C$

The first line contains the major premise. The second line contains the minor premise. The last line is called the conclusion. Notice that when making an argument, you have to have something that links the propositions together. What do I mean by this? To get to the conclusion (that $A = C$), I have to have something to link A and C together; after all, that is what my conclusion is claiming. What is it that links A and C together? It is B. B is called the middle term, and it has to be distributed (which means it has to occur in both premises) to link the argument together properly. Confused on that part? Don't be confused; we are going to clarify this as we go.

Truth, Validity, and Soundness

To make an argument you need true premises that are linked together correctly.

True statements + a correct structure = a good argument. But the way we analyze the premises is different from the way we analyze how they are linked (the structure).

These three terms: truth, validity, and soundness are often used interchangeably in common speech. But in logic, they have very specific meanings. Truth deals with *propositions*. Validity deals with logical *structure*. Soundness deals with *arguments*. To say it another way, full-blown arguments are not true; only premises are true. Premises are not valid; only structures are valid. *Truth*, *validity*, and *soundness* are technical terms in logic that refer to different things. Allow me to elaborate on each one to further explain.

A sentence can be either true or false:

> My name is Zach.
> The sky is purple.
> Pirates are really cool.

Even if we don't *know* whether a proposition is true or false, if it is an actual proposition (and not a logical contradiction or a sentence that is not really a statement), then it is either true or false. Notice that you can have true propositions that don't make an argument:

> My name is Zach.
> George Washington was the first president of the United States.
> _____
> Therefore, two plus two equals four.

Every statement in this syllogism is true. However, it doesn't actually make an argument because the sentences don't support each other properly. An argument can't just have true propositions; the propositions actually have to align correctly. This is called validity.

Validity has to do with the logical structure of an argument. *When talking about validity all we are interested in is the structure.* An argument can be valid in its structure even if the propositions it uses are false. Let me give you an example:

> If monsters exist, then the moon is made of cheese.
> Monsters do exist.
>
> ———————
>
> Therefore, the moon is made of cheese.

Notice that the structure of this argument is completely valid. Now, the propositions aren't true, but we are not worried about that here. Truth has to do with propositions, and all we care about at this exact moment is structure (i.e., validity). The structure is completely valid. It is not saying that monsters actually exist or that the moon is actually made of cheese. It is simply saying that *if* one were true, *then* the other would follow. The structure is valid because it looks like this:

> If A, then B
> A
>
> ———————
>
> Therefore, B

Let's look at another argument that I heard my friend's two-year-old son say:

> A T-Rex has sharp teeth.
> I have sharp teeth.
>
> ———————
>
> Therefore, I am a T-Rex.

What is wrong with this argument? It is true that a T-Rex does have sharp teeth. And it is true that my buddy's son has sharp teeth (kids' teeth are notoriously sharp). But notice that the last statement, the conclusion, is not true. Why? *The structure of the argument makes a mistake.* The first line says that the category of T-Rexes fits into the category of things with sharp teeth (which is true) but notice that the opposite is not true. It is not the case that everything in the category of things with sharp teeth fits into the category of things that are T-Rexes. There are a lot of things with sharp teeth that are not dinosaurs (e.g., sharks, snakes, tigers, saws, and my friend's child).

If an argument has both true premises and a valid structure, it is called a sound argument. So, to summarize everything thus far:

> Propositions can be true or false.
> Structures can be valid or invalid.
> Arguments can be sound or unsound.

I say all of that to simply make this point: If you have true premises and a valid structure, *then the argument is sound whether you want to believe it or not!* You are not allowed to disagree with an argument that has true premises and a valid structure and still be considered a rational person. If you believe that an argument is unsound, you must show that it has at least one false premise or has a structural deficiency.

Our whole life should be about finding and holding to sound arguments. True premises plus a valid structure equals a sound (and therefore binding) argument.

Rules for Categorical Syllogisms[3]

1. The middle term must be distributed at least once.
2. If a term is distributed in the conclusion, then it must be distributed in the premise.

3. Two negative premises are not allowed.
4. A negative premise requires a negative conclusion, and a negative conclusion requires a negative premise.
5. If both premises are universal, the conclusion cannot be particular.

All those rules sound a bit sterile, so let's look at some practical examples of syllogisms gone wrong and see if we can spot the errors. You'll need to read this next part slowly, but if you get what is being said, you are on your way to thinking clearly.

Mistakes

Let's look at some examples of mistakes that are often made in syllogistic reasoning. Most of these arguments will seem kind of ridiculous, but our job is to see *why* they are ridiculous.

> All horses are black.
> There is a horse.
> _____
> Therefore, it must be black.

The problem with this syllogism is that it has a false premise. The first premise is not true. Not all horses are black, and therefore the argument fails. But notice that the structure is valid. *Had the first premise been true, then the argument would have worked.*

Had we said:

> All horses are animals.
> There is a horse.
> _____
> Therefore, it is an animal.

That would have been an absolutely great argument. It has true premises and a valid structure, so it is sound. But, because the original syllogism had a false premise, the argument (about all horses being black) is not sound. If one premise is off in a chain of reasoning, then the entire chain becomes suspect.

Let's look at another syllogism:

All men are humans.
All women are humans.
_____
Therefore, all men are women.

Notice that the first two premises are true. Both men and women (and all of them) are humans. Why does the argument fail? Why is it unsound? Well, because the argument is invalid; its structure is not correct. It first states that all men are in the category of humans and all women are in the category of humans (so far so good). But it then makes the radical statement that men and women are therefore in the exact same (smaller) category just because they are in the same larger category. But that is not true. There can be two subclasses in a larger category that are not, themselves, a part of each other. Imagine one big circle labeled "humans," and within this big circle there are two smaller circles that are not touching each another. One of these smaller circles is labeled "men," and the other is labeled "women." This syllogism fails because it acts like, just because the two small circles are in the big circle, then they must also be inside each other or overlapping.

Or consider:

All murder is killing.
All murder is bad.
_____
Therefore, all killing is bad.

Notice the mistake here. The first two premises say something about murder that is true. Murder does involve killing, and murder is, indeed, bad. But the argument only says that murder is both "killing" and "bad." This does not mean that all killing is bad. The syllogism makes no argument at all about killing in war or self-defense, for example. The argument only states that one kind of killing is bad (i.e., "murder"). This syllogism breaks Rule 2. Notice the term that is distributed in the premise (*murder*) does not occur at all in the conclusion. Premise one is about murder. Premise two is about murder. But then the term *murder* doesn't even occur in the conclusion, so the syllogism fails.

What about this one?

> No birds are cats.
> No cats can fly.
> _____
> Therefore, no birds can fly.

This breaks Rule 3. You cannot draw conclusions based on two negative premises. If you ask me, "What is a crocodile like?" and I say, "It is not an airplane and it is not a wheel of cheese," that doesn't help you very much. All this syllogism says is that if you have a circle labeled "cats," there won't be any circle labeled "birds" in it. And it you have that same circle labeled "cats," there won't be a circle labeled "things that can fly" in it. This does not mean that there cannot be a circle labeled "birds" within the "things-that-can-fly" circle!

Or consider:

> Some cats are not black.
> Some black things are not cats.
> _____
> Therefore, some cats are black.

The conclusion is true. Some cats do happen to be black. But the argument as a whole is unsound. This syllogism says that some cats are not black (which is true), and it says that some black things (like coal) are not cats (which is also true). However, just because we say some cats are not black *that does not allow us to necessarily infer that some cats are black*. Most students have trouble with this example, so let me say it again by using the exact same argument, but we will replace the word *black* with the word *clear*. Consider:

> Some cats are not clear.
> Some clear things are not cats.
> _____
> Therefore, some cats *are* clear.

You see why this argument fails. You cannot have a negative premise without having a negative conclusion and vice versa. The first premise ("Some cats are not clear") is true because no cats are clear. The second premise is true. Some clear things such as windows are not cats (because no windows are cats). But neither of these implies that some cats *are* indeed clear.

We could list 100 more syllogisms, and we could get really technical. We could talk more about the difference between affirmative and negative premises. We could talk more about the difference between universal and particular statements. We could talk about conversion, contradiction, subalternation, etc. We could draw a lot of charts and diagrams. But you can go to any logic textbook to find that helpful and necessary information. That is not the purpose of this book. This book is written for the average person. *I have found that it is more helpful to teach people to learn to see what is wrong (even if they don't have all the names and charts and such), rather than having them memorize paradigms (only to forget them later).* To say it another way, I want to teach you to think critically and to understand why syllogisms fail even if you don't know all the technical terminology. Anytime you see an argument, you should be able to see what is going wrong just by thinking about it.

Keep it simple. When you read or hear an argument, simply ask yourself, "Why does this seem wrong?"

The bottom line is this: *If there is an argument with all true premises and a valid structure, then the argument is sound, and you must accept it. If you don't want to accept it, then you have to show where a premise is false or where the structure is invalid.*

To give a final example, let me briefly use the famous "ontological argument" for God's existence. The argument is too complicated to fully explain here. Essentially, it is an argument that proves God's existence just from what we mean by the word *God*. It states that God is a necessarily existent being and to think of God as not existing is not to be thinking about the Christian God at all. The argument can be stated like this:

> God is a being greater than which none can be thought.
>
> To be a being greater than which none can be thought would include actually existing (because the thought of an actually existing God is greater than the thought of a God who might not exist).

> ———————

> Therefore, God exists.

Now, the argument is not claiming that if you can think of something great, it must exist. That would be ridiculous. The argument is showing that there is a logical contradiction in the mind of the person who says that (1) they are really thinking about God and (2) they are also thinking that he may not exist. You cannot think of God as a being greater-than-which-none-can-be-thought and also think that he might not exist.

Confused yet? Let me make it as clear as I can. Imagine that I said, "Think of a triangle." That seems simple enough. Now imagine that you said you were thinking of a triangle, but that the triangle you were thinking about didn't have three sides. Well, then you have contradicted yourself. You were clearly not thinking of a triangle. You can't say that you are thinking of a triangle and also say that you don't think it has three sides. If you think both of those thoughts at the same time, you have committed a contradiction.

The same is true with the ontological argument. If I ask you to think of the greatest possible being (which you can do), but you also think that this being might not exist, you are not thinking of the greatest possible being. You are contradicting yourself. You cannot think of a triangle and also not think that it has three sides. You cannot think of a mountain range without also thinking of valleys. And you cannot think of a being greater-than-which-none-can-be-thought and also think of that being as possibly not existing.

Here is what is amazing about the ontological argument. Both its premises are true, and its structure is valid. Therefore, it is sound. It might not convert the most hardened atheist, but that is only because they don't like the argument, not because the argument doesn't work.

Learning about true premises, valid structures, and sound arguments matters in the Christian life.

There is a famous story about the atheist philosopher Bertrand Russell walking around a college campus thinking about the ontological argument. At one point he threw his pipe tobacco up in the air and exclaimed, "The ontological argument is sound! . . . But unpersuasive." My question to Russell would be, "If it has true premises and a valid structure, why is the argument unpersuasive?" What could be more persuasive than a sound argument?

Perhaps one's presuppositions and worldview can sometimes make one less logical than they pretend to be. Perhaps we suppress truths we don't like when they don't confirm our already established worldview.

Hidden Premises

Many arguments contain hidden premises. That is, the argument has a built-in proposition that is not stated explicitly. These arguments are tricky.

Pretend that you are a single guy on a date with an attractive girl. Though you think the date is going well, she says she doesn't want to see you again. Heartbroken, you ask why. She says, "You're not really my type." You reply, "What is your type?" And she says, "Handsome."

That's pretty crushing. If I had a nickel for every time this has happened to me, I would have three nickels. I'm kidding of course; that has never happened to me (and I wouldn't tell you if it had). But you can see why the young man felt a sick burn.

Although the girl in our example didn't express her reason explicitly, she did imply it. The augment would look something like this:

> I only date people who are my type.
>
> My type is people who are attractive.
>
> You are not attractive (hidden premise).

Therefore, I do not want to date you anymore.

Remember, language can be tricky, and people often imply things that they don't say explicitly. This is not necessarily a fallacy or a bad thing. We imply premises all the time. You just have to be aware that it is happening.

CHAPTER 9

causation

This chapter may seem a little random. Most logic books don't have a chapter on causation. Why am I including it here? Because it serves as an excellent transition chapter before we get into the second half of the book, which is all about logical fallacies.

I have heard people say that their spouse "caused" them to commit adultery. I have heard people say that someone "caused" their coworker to commit suicide. I have heard people say that violent video games "caused" a person to go on a shooting spree. I have heard people say that trying alcohol "caused" them to become a drunkard. These illogical examples show why talking about causation may help us be better thinkers.

Basically, the whole point of this section is to get you to think really hard about the concept of causation. There is not a ton of traditional logic here, but you will need to know this philosophical concept if you are going to think critically.

Let me give you this scenario:

> Let's say a man named Bob shoots a man named
> Mike from 10 feet away, and Mike dies. What *caused*
> Mike's death?

Think about it for a second.

Perhaps you say that the *gun* caused Mike's death. But how could that happen? The gun is 10 feet away from Mike and never comes any closer to him than that. So, the gun could not *cause* Mike's death.

Maybe you say the *bullet* is what killed Mike. It can't be the gun because the gun is just a launching pad for the bullet. Perhaps it really is the projectile that killed Mike. But that can't be right either. How can a piece of metal, flying through the air, necessarily cause someone's death? A bullet is just a tiny piece of metal that doesn't hurt anyone unless it is made to do so. A little piece of metal doesn't inherently take someone's life and cause their soul to leave their body. In fact, people get shot all the time and don't die.

So maybe it was the *propellant* that killed Mike. The bullet would have never gotten to him (or gone through his body) unless there was some type of propellant. But we don't think the gunpowder really killed Mike, do we? When there is a mass shooting, people don't try to have the government restrict the ancient chemical compound known as gunpowder. Additionally, even if a bullet is launched by propellant and goes directly through your body *that doesn't necessarily kill you.* It doesn't kill you when it goes through your finger, for example. It would have to hit the central nervous system or cut an artery or something to kill you.

"Oh," you may say, "I see now . . . *blood loss* is what killed Mike." But that's not right either. Blood loss wouldn't kill you if there was a way to keep oxygenated blood going up to your brain.

We lose blood every time we fall and skin our knee. So perhaps *the loss of oxygenated blood to the brain* killed Mike. But if all that is true, then why do we charge Bob with the crime? Bob didn't make oxygenated blood stop going to Mike's brain. All Bob did was pull a trigger . . .

You see, causation, like language, can be very tricky. What *caused* Mike's death?

> Bob
> The gun
> The propellant
> The bullet
> Good aim
> The loss of blood
> The loss of oxygen to the brain
> The fact that Mike is mortal
> The fall of man from Genesis 3
> God's providence

All of these are the right answer depending on what you mean by "cause."[1]

A similar pattern happened during the COVID-19 pandemic in 2020. People said that COVID-19 "caused" the death of many people. But what do we mean by "caused"? If someone had heart disease and they caught the virus and died, did COVID-19 kill them, or did their unhealthy heart kill them? In what way did the virus affect their heart? If someone who was severely obese died after contracting COVID-19, did the virus "cause" their death? Or did their lack of exercise, clogged arteries, weak lungs, or 30 years of bad decisions cause their death? We don't have time to answer all these things here. Suffice it to say that we need to do more thinking about what *cause* means before we make grandiose claims using that word.

Aristotle

Aristotle recognized that we can be talking about very different things when we are using the word *cause*. So, he distinguished between four types of cause:

> Material Cause
> Formal Cause
> Efficient Cause
> Final Cause

As I said earlier, causation is complicated, and we could say a lot about it, but let me try to make it as simple as possible. Let's say that we want to build a train with a steam engine. What is the "cause" of this train? Well, the *material* cause is what the train is made of—metal. Metal, in a sense, causes the train to be a train. If there was no metal, the train would not be strong enough to pull its cargo and get from point A to point B. Trains made of paper don't work very well. But just having a chunk of metal is not a train. A paperweight can be a chunk of metal, but it is not a train. It needs to be in the shape of a train. The metal has to be in the *form* of a train. There have to be blueprints that help us make the train into the shape of a train. The blueprint (the form) is also the cause of a train—the *formal* cause.

But we are not done yet. There is also the *efficient* cause. There has to be someone who directly causes the train to be built. Workers have to forge the metal, drive in the bolts, and attach the coal tinder. That is what is known as the efficient cause of the train. Science, for example, is primarily concerned with efficient causes. Last and most important, there is the *final* cause of the train. A train has to be designed *for something*. In this case the train is to get cargo and passengers from one location to another. You must have the desire of the train builder to have a train for some purpose. *You see, none of the other causes matter if you don't have a final cause.* Nobody mines for iron, nobody draws up blueprints, nobody builds railroads, and nobody puts the train together without the original plan and purpose for a train.

So, going back to our previous example, we ask again, "What *caused* Mike's death?" The efficient cause was the lack of oxygenated blood going to the brain. But the final cause was Bob.

Why do I say all this technical stuff about cause? *The simple reason is that people misuse the word* cause *all the time. So anytime you hear the word* cause, *you should stop and ask, "What do they mean by 'cause'?"*

But we run into another issue when it comes to causation, and it is an issue brought to our attention by the genius congenial skeptic David Hume.

Hume

There is much we could say about Hume but, for the purpose of this chapter, we will stick to his skepticism of causation. Hume pointed out that almost all our knowledge is based upon our idea of causation. But, and here is where it gets sticky, we don't *experience* causation.

That is huge.

For Hume, there are two ways of knowing (called Hume's fork). These two ways are "relations of ideas" and "matters of fact." Relations of ideas are similar to our discussion of deduction in Chapter 7. They are things we can know intuitively without doing experiments. We can know that $2 + 2 = 4$ and that all triangles have angles that equal 180 degrees just by thinking of these concepts. However, *causation* is not like that. Causation is not a relation of ideas. It, therefore, must be something we *experience*. It must be the other prong of Hume's fork. It must be a matter of fact. A matter of fact is similar to our discussion of induction. It is something that we know from experience and not something that is intuitive.

But now we run into a problem: Our knowledge of causation seems to be neither. It seems like we know causation neither as a relation of ideas nor as a matter of fact. We don't know it before experience (*a priori*) or after experience (*a posteriori*). It is not something we know intuitively (like math), and it is not something we know from experience (like counting crows); *we have never experienced causation.*

We experience one billiard ball hitting another, and we experience the second billiard ball moving, but *we do not actually see the cause.* We only see one ball move and another ball move. "But," you may say, "what do you mean that we don't see the first ball *cause* the other ball to move . . . it *has to* move!" But, as many a philosophy professor has pointed out to students, you never actually experience this "*has to.*" Imagine this scene: Adam and Eve are in the garden, and they have just been created when someone hits one billiard ball toward another one. They have *no idea* what is going to happen to the second ball. Maybe it will explode. Maybe it will bounce back. Maybe it will pop up into the air. They don't know. There is nothing *intrinsic* in the first billiard ball that requires that the second one acts the way it does!

Hume basically lets us know that we have no reason for all our practical knowledge (which is based on causation). For Hume, our knowledge is not really knowledge, it is just an irrational habit that we have created by nature.

I say all this weird stuff about Hume to say two things. First, *causation* is a very tricky topic. People use that term all the time and have no idea what they mean.

Second, without God, Hume may be right. David Hume, who was an atheist, thought that all our knowledge of science was not really knowledge at all. Don't get me wrong; science works. It works great. But Hume would say we don't know *why* it works. We just think the future will be like the past just because we have experienced it to be like the past before (which is a logical fallacy). For Hume, human science was just as magical as voodoo. If there is no God, then Hume may be correct. If there is no God who allows us to understand causation (and, therefore, the world around us) then we really have lost all scientific and objective knowledge. God allows us to better explain what we mean by the concept of causation.

The idea that we have no knowledge is scary. But having a non-Christian view of causation may lead to that very conclusion. But Hume gets even worse.

Imagine for example that everything is material. There is no God; there are no souls; there are no angels; only material objects exist. Well, if this is the case, then how can we escape strict determinism? How can we escape the idea that everything has to happen exactly the way it did? If one atom moves another atom and that atom causes another to move and that atom causes another to move, then everything that happens *has* to happen exactly that way that it does. *Humans really have no such thing as any type of morality or "free will" if everything is physical.* If that sounds too complicated, let me give you an example of what I mean. If Bob kills Mike, we hold Bob responsible. Why do we hold him responsible? Well, because he could have *not* killed Mike. But if everything is physically caused (nothing exists except matter), then Bob *had to* murder Mike. He didn't really have a choice. One atom moved another atom that moved another atom that changed a chemical in Bob's brain that caused his hand to move that caused him to point a gun at Mike and caused him to pull the trigger. You see, without God you are stuck between a few strange options when it comes to causation:

> You can say that we have no real knowledge because we don't experience causation (Hume).

> You can say that we help frame your own world, *though you can never experience the actual object* devoid of the space and time you lay over reality (Kant).[2]

> Or you can say that everything has to happen exactly as it does, and human choice is an illusion (materialism).

But the existence of God allows you to avoid all these strange conclusions. He allows you to give an account for knowledge, objectivity, causation, and morality.

The bottom line is this: Causation is a very difficult topic. Any time someone says one thing caused another, we must pause to see exactly what they are saying. Did one thing *necessarily* cause another? Did it just influence another? What is the ultimate cause of the event? Could the event have happened without the alleged cause?

Cause is one of those words that should pop out to you anytime you hear it in an argument.

PART II:

Logical Fallacies

This section is the most enjoyable part of the book because we get to make fun of people (including ourselves)!

Logical fallacies are mistakes in reasoning that we all make from time to time. There are different ways to classify fallacies (e.g., formal, linguistic, material, etc.), but all that is going to be extra-confusing stuff that you don't really need to know. The most important exercise we can do is to list the name of a logical fallacy, explain what it is, and then give several examples of where we see that fallacy—both in our culture and in the church. This is, after all, a book on logic for Christians.

It can be easy to become cynical as we read through a huge list of mistakes in reasoning. You have probably heard many of the fallacies I mention below made by your pastor, friend, family member, favorite politician, or celebrity hero. So, I would encourage you to read through the examples with some humility. We all make mistakes in our reasoning from time to time.

Hopefully, we can learn from these negative examples so that we become better thinkers in the future.

It is okay to point out the flaws in others and to know that you are right on an issue. That is not arrogance. Arrogance is a matter of the heart, not a matter of thinking critically. I will be the first to admit that I have committed every single one of these fallacies and probably commit several each day. But, hopefully, by studying these mistakes, we can avoid poor reasoning in our own lives and avoid being seduced by the bad arguments of others.

Disclaimer

Part II of this book deals with some very controversial social, moral, and political issues. Abortion, homosexuality, feminism, gun control, global warming, and other "hot topics" are mentioned throughout this section. My fear is that someone will assume that I'm using these topics to "shame" or "dismiss" people who might disagree with me. I assure you that is not my intent.

This is a book on logic, so I am unable to go into depth on every issue. What might feel like a "drive-by" on a very controversial issue is really just my attempt to point out how those who support that issue often employ a mistake in reasoning. It is not my attempt to actually shepherd that person in this short book. For example, if I show that it is a fallacy (on the abortion issue) to claim that one's baby is just a part of one's body, that doesn't mean that I don't care for those struggling with the aftermath of an abortion. If I mention a mistake made in reasoning by the LGBTQ lobby, that does not mean that I am seeking to dismiss the question of how Christians should relate to those who are same-sex attracted or who experience gender dysphoria. If I mention "gun control," that does not mean that I do or do not think you should own a gun. This section only deals with logical fallacies; it does not deal with the broad topic of other issues.

This section isn't designed to fully deal with those big issues; it is only a place to deal with some errors in thinking about those issues. Therefore, I've included a link to our church's website where you can access hour-long lessons on almost all the controversial issues I mention. Using this additional resource will allow you to go into detail on an issue without feeling as though I unfairly dismissed it:

https://www.theparkwaychurch.com/tecrecordings

Equivocation

If you remember only one logical fallacy, remember what an equivocation is. I would say that probably 95 percent of all logical mistakes fall under the category of equivocation. An equivocation is where you use the same word in two (or more) different ways without clearly distinguishing that you are doing so. It is the most popular fallacy—by far.

In fact, several jokes are based on equivocation. For example, what do you call the guy who edited Hitler's speeches?

A grammar Nazi.

This is an example of equivocation. The word *Nazi* can be used for a national socialist in the 1930s and 1940s, but it can be used for someone who is really a stickler for the rules.

You see this fallacy all the time in churches. Someone will say that you shouldn't do church discipline or that parents shouldn't spank their kids because it is not "loving." That is the fallacy of equivocation. *Doing what the Bible commands you to do is always loving.* "Loving" is not defined by what you and I *think* is loving; it is defined as what the Bible says is loving. In this example, people are using the word *loving* in a different way than the Bible uses it. That is an equivocation. Church discipline (Matt. 18; 1 Cor. 5) and spanking (Prov. 13:24; 19:18; 20:30; 22:15; 23:13–14; 29:15, 17;) are both the loving thing to do.

When someone says that you should not "judge" them (despite the fact that the Bible actually tells Christians to judge one another in 1 Corinthians 5:12), they are committing an equivocation. What they often mean when they say that you shouldn't judge them is that you shouldn't tell them that some sin they are committing is wrong. But that's not what judging means in the context of the Sermon on the Mount (or else Jesus broke this command every time he rebuked the Pharisees). Rather, what the Bible forbids is *hypocritical* judging. It does not forbid all judging of any kind. It forbids the kind of judging where the person with the plank in their eye corrects the person with only a speck in their eye (Matt. 7:1–5). Again, we have to watch out for the fallacy of equivocation.

How many Christians sit down to debate whether or not humans have free will and never stop and identify what the heck they mean by the term *free will*? By free will, the Arminian means something like, "a will that can freely choose between two options" or "a will that can choose against its nature." For the

Calvinist, free will means something like, "a will that can freely choose only in accordance with one's highest desires." Until you define which definition you're talking about, talking about free will is a useless exercise.

Understanding the fallacy of equivocation also solves the problem between why Paul can say that one is saved by faith alone and James seems to say we are saved by works. These two biblical authors are not contradicting each other. They are using the same word, *faith*, in two different ways.[1] James is not saying that you are saved by something other than mere trust in Jesus. He is critiquing those who say they have faith but only have the same kind of mental ascent that the demons have.

Paul is using the word *faith* to mean true faith. James is using the word *faith* to mean mere verbal ascent but with no real quality to it (and hence no life change). So, they don't contradict each other. They are just using the word *faith* in different ways to mean different things. They both believe one is justified by faith alone. But the kind of faith that justifies is never alone. There is no contradiction. We only think there is a contradiction because we equivocate on the word *faith*.

As I'm writing this there is a huge debate raging in Evangelicalism over "justice." After all, Christians are supposed to support justice. But before we can support justice, we have to define *justice*. Is social justice the same thing as biblical justice? Is it unjust for God to give some people 10 talents and only give another person 5 talents (and tell them to be content with what they have)? Do people cry for justice if a criminal is murdered by a police officer but not if a police officer is murdered by a criminal? Is the fact that wealth is not distributed evenly a form of injustice? Or is injustice only when one does not have the same equality before the law (under the Constitution)? We certainly cannot answer all these things here. Suffice it to say that *if we were more aware of equivocation, we could avoid some of the craziness that divides Christian churches.*

Let me give one more example just to continue beating this dead horse. Parents who have a child that practices homosexuality have asked me: "Can we attend our son's gay wedding?" Well, the reason this question comes up is because of equivocation. Parents are equivocating on the word *wedding*. Parents know that they should attend their child's wedding, so when they skip out on their son's wedding (to another man), they feel bad. But should they feel bad? What if there is no such thing as a *gay wedding*? A *wedding*, by definition, is between a man and a woman. So, if we rephrase the question without the equivocation it becomes, "Can we attend a celebration of our son's sin of homosexuality?" Well, now the question is easier to answer. We have to watch out for equivocation. The word *wedding* is being used in two different ways, which is why this question even comes up. Don't get me wrong. We are to love, care for, and befriend those who practice homosexuality. There is no sin that cannot be covered by Jesus's blood if one will repent. But we are not to support sin. As the old adage goes, "Love the sinner and hate the sin."

So, the next time something seems confusing or a biblical passage seems to contradict another one or you are arguing with someone, stop and ask, "In what ways might I be experiencing an equivocation? In what ways are we using the same word with slightly different meanings?"

False Dichotomy

A false dichotomy is pretty simple. It is when one acts like there are only two options when there are other options.

We see this all the time. It is used in courtrooms, churches, schools, and advertising.

"There are some things money can't buy, for everything else, there's Mastercard."

See the false dichotomy there? You have two options: priceless things or using Mastercard.

But what if I want to use Visa or cash? What if I want to use rubles or pesos? What if I want to use euros or pounds? What about non-priceless things?

This fallacy occurs a lot in theology as well. "Do you believe the earth is young or old?" Well, maybe I hold a nuanced position; maybe there are more options. Or someone will ask you, "Is God sovereign, or do we make real, meaningful decisions?" Why does it have to be one or the other?

Whenever you are given only a few options, stop and ask yourself, "Are there any other possibilities here?"

The devil even tries to use a false dichotomy on Jesus. He tells him that, if he is really God's Son, he should throw himself off the pinnacle of the temple. Notice the two choices: Either test God or show that you're not the eternal Son of God. But Jesus doesn't play into the trap. He remains faithful to God (thus showing he is the Messiah) and also doesn't put God to the test.

I heard a guy who is a pastor recently say that if Christians want to outlaw abortion, we need to be willing to adopt all the unwanted babies. If we are not willing to adopt them, then we can't make abortion illegal.

That is a false dichotomy.

With this fallacy, people are literally saying that there are times when you should not oppose murdering babies. Would we hold this for any other issue? Would we say that we should not outlaw rape unless we are willing to have all those assaulted women move into our homes? You don't only have two options here. You should outlaw abortion, *and* you should care for those who need help. But one doesn't cancel out the other. Even if no babies were ever adopted ever again, abortion should still be illegal.

If someone is being physically abused in their marriage, they often think that they only have two options: to continue being abused or to get divorced. But why are those the only two options? What about getting away physically (for a time), so you are not getting abused, but then getting counseling with your spouse through your local church so that your marriage can be redeemed?

Bottom Line: When someone gives you a few options, always see if there are more.

Appeal to Emotion (*ad misericordiam*)

Now you know the logic is getting good because I'm starting to give you fancy Latin names for some of these fallacies. An *ad misericordiam* is where one appeals to emotion instead of the facts of what is being debated. You see the term *misery* in this fallacy's Latin title because it tries to provoke feelings of empathy.

Have you ever seen that commercial where they show a bunch of sad-looking dogs locked up in cages? They play Sarah McLachlan's "I Will Remember You" as they scan the camera on dogs that look sickly and injured. Their hope is that this emotional display will make you want to adopt the puppies. That is an appeal to emotion. Now, don't get me wrong, if you want to adopt a puppy, go for it.[2] But you should have a *reason* to adopt one, and that reason should not just be because someone is pulling your heartstrings on a TV commercial.

Anytime someone uses a story to evoke emotion instead of making a logical case, you have to be on guard against an appeal to emotion. Statements such as "You don't know what I've been through," "Think about how hard that will be for that person," or "That just doesn't feel right to me" often appeal (errantly) to the emotions.

There are appropriate times to consider one's emotions. Emotions are not bad. A good rhetorician should be able to provoke emotions within his listening audience. What is bad, though, is when *reason is ignored, and the whole argument is just emotion.* Things are true regardless of how we feel about them. Facts don't care about your feelings.

Someone might tell you that drinking is a sin and, when you ask them why they think that, they go on to describe all the terrible, abusive things their alcoholic father did to them when they were a child. Now, it's terrible that that happened to them, and I don't want to minimize their trauma, *but their emotional experience is irrelevant to whether or not drinking is sinful as defined by scripture.*

This fallacy can easily be committed in a culture with a heightened "victimization" mentality. We can assume that whoever gives the best sob story must be right. Again, we want to care for those who are truly victims. *But we only know who victims are by looking at truth*, not by looking at emotion. Leviticus 19:15 says, "You shall do no injustice in court. You shall not be partial to the poor or defer to the great, but in righteousness shall you judge your neighbor." Notice that we are not to give any partiality based on misery, emotion, past defeats, power differences, or a difficult situation. We are on the side of truth, no matter what. Sometimes, the victim is the person who claims to be the victim. Sometimes, the person who claims to be the victim is actually the victimizer and is using the title of "victim" as a mask to disguise their evil behavior.

Attacking the Person *(ad hominem)*

This is an incredibly common logical fallacy: Instead of critiquing someone's argument, you just attack the person or their character. This is probably the second most common logical fallacy after equivocation.

When someone in politics says, "My opponent doesn't support this political bill, but he's an awful person, so we can all ignore him." That is an example of an *ad hominem*. They haven't actually addressed the arguments against the political bill being proposed; they have ignored logic and moved on to attacking the person. People often don't deal with the actual arguments and policies put forward by a political candidate because it is easier to just attack their character. But here is the kicker: Their argument might be right even if they are a scumbag. Regardless of the *person,* you should address the *policy.*

Name-calling works that way in our society. Instead of addressing someone's argument, it's easier to attack them with names such as "bigot," "racist," "homophobe," "Nazi," "idiot," etc. But that doesn't deal with the issues. Regardless of how crazy we think someone is, we have to show *why* they are crazy and, to do that, we have to use logic.

If Osama bin Laden were making a case that two plus two equals four, would the fact that he was a notorious terrorist mean he was wrong in that claim? The answer is no. Of course, he was an evil, terrible person—don't get me wrong. But if you thought that two plus two actually equaled five, you would have to prove it in some way other than talking about how bad bin Laden was.

If a serial adulterer were to say that adultery is bad. Is he right? He is right! Yes, he's a hypocrite, but he is a hypocrite who is correct. We are not free to dismiss his claim just because of his character.

You see this same fallacy used sometimes in theology. Someone will say that Martin Luther wrote some works that were anti-Semitic, so we shouldn't read the other things he wrote. Or they will say that John Calvin allowed a guy to be burned at the stake, so he obviously wasn't a good theologian. Or they will say that Jonathan Edwards owned slaves, so he obviously must be wrong on his view of salvation. But is this type of thinking logical? Does the fact that someone has a character flaw mean we cannot or should not listen to *anything* they say? Would you say that the civil rights leader Martin Luther King Jr. should not have advocated for equal rights for African Americans because, in his personal life, he was a serial adulterer and denied the Trinity?[3] I would say we should listen to Luther, Calvin, Edwards, and King Jr. *in the areas where they were right* and simply repudiate the areas where they were wrong. The flaws in their character don't affect the soundness of their positions.

However, this does not mean that all critiques of character are irrelevant. There is a right way to critique someone's character in particular situations. Say there is a felon who was locked up for murder and he wants to become a babysitter. In this case you *can* use his (bad) character to deny him that position. However, notice that you *are actually making an argument here* (and thus not committing the *ad hominem* fallacy). You are implying that "since this man has a history of violence, he might be violent again, and therefore, should not be allowed to watch children."

Notice how this example took into account the felon's character, but his character is not the ultimate reason why he couldn't be a babysitter. An actual argument still had to be made about how he might act in the future based on how he acted in the past. So, we *can* consider character and how that might affect a decision, but we cannot *substitute* that for making a logical case.

Appeal to the Wrong Authority (*ad verecundiam*)

This fallacy occurs when, instead of building an argument or critiquing an opposing argument using logic, one appeals to a supposed "authority" on the subject (who isn't actually an authority on that particular subject).

Some people misunderstand this logical fallacy, so follow me closely here: It is not wrong, in some cases, to appeal to authority. If someone wanted to prove that the Bible teaches that some action is a sin, then appealing to the Bible is totally valid. If someone wanted to show the meaning of something in the Constitution by appealing to other documents written by the founding fathers, then they have not committed this fallacy. If someone wanted to make a case that a particular virus will make you sick, then they are allowed to appeal to the opinion of doctors. We are not against all appeals to authority. We are just against *errant* appeals to authority. That's what the *ad verecundiam* fallacy is all about.

So, if you want to make an argument about how to dunk a basketball, then Lebron James is a great authority to whom you can appeal. However, if Lebron James was on an insurance commercial telling you where you should get your medical coverage, then he has stepped out of bounds (pun intended). He is not an expert on insurance law. He is not an expert on deductibles and premiums. In this example, an *ad verecundiam* is being committed because the insurance commercial appeals to an errant authority. They are trying to get you to think that their insurance is great because they paid a professional basketball player to say it's great.

Scientists are usually not competent to judge matters of religion or theology. Mathematicians are usually not experts on morality. Lawyers are usually not experts on the best way to crochet a blanket. You can use authorities, but you just can't misuse them. You have to use the right authorities on the right topics.

You see this fallacy every time an entertainer gives their opinions on politics. Why on earth should we care what Beyoncé or Brad Pitt or Kim Kardashian or Madonna thinks about political and social issues? Why do we care what Bill Nye, who actually doesn't have the requisite academic training in science, thinks about the electoral college? All these are appeals to the wrong authority—*ad verecundiam* arguments.

You see this fallacy in church as well. People will often appeal to some supposed "Bible teacher" (who you have never heard of) to support some strange reading of scripture. People will appeal to "prophecy experts" who come up with interpretations of the book of Revelation that no one in all church history has ever held. People will say, "I know the Bible says you should physically discipline your children . . . but some secular psychologist, with no training in theology, says that discipline will hurt their self-esteem."

Whenever someone tells me that God "told" them the meaning of some biblical text, I say, "Well, he told me it means the exact opposite." Now what do we do? How do we know who's right? We have to get rid of the fallacy of appealing to an errant authority (in this case a misunderstanding of where meaning is found and how God speaks to us) and see who can make the best case for the actual, historical-grammatical meaning of the biblical text.

We have to have humility. None of us is an expert on everything. I saw an attorney who had a mug that said, "Don't confuse your Google search with my law degree." I love that. Wikipedia, YouTube, and mom-blogs are not real authorities, and you should not appeal to them 99.99 percent of the time. Have humility to know where you are untrained, and don't pretend to be an expert where you are not.

The whole anti-vaccine movement became a worldwide phenomenon based on this fallacy. A doctor who had his medical license revoked and a former porn star somehow convinced millions of people, despite the overwhelming opinion of the scientific community, that we should stop vaccinating our kids. The result is not only outbreaks of almost eradicated diseases in the United States but in third-world countries as well. Regardless of what you think about the vaccine issue, you have to admit that most anti-vaxxers appeal to authorities that are not true authorities in that field. Quoting conspiracy theory websites online is not the same as doing your PhD in chemistry or infectious disease.

We can often appeal to authorities to help us solve issues—but not always. What do you do when the experts disagree? What do you do when an expert is wrong? Well, logic ultimately trumps expertise. Expertise is helpful, but it is not definitive.

In summary, using logic to make a good argument is what ultimately decides who is right. You can sometimes appeal to authorities (depending on the authority and the argument being made). However, you should never appeal to a *wrong* authority, no matter how popular they are, to bolster your case.

Category Mistake

This one may seem a little tricky but, if you have kids, you already know what a category mistake is.

"Daddy, what color is time?"

That's a pretty difficult question! What color *is* time? Time doesn't have a color. (Though if a boy is asking the question, I'll probably just say blue, and if a girl is asking the question, I'll probably just say pink.) That very question is a category mistake. The category of color is being read onto the category of time.

This fallacy is made anytime something in one category is placed into a category where it does not belong.

This often happens in politics when the role of the church is confused with the role of the state. When discussing some political issue, Christians will often say something like, "We should (fill in the blank)." However, they don't stop and clearly articulate who the "we" is in their sentence. When they say, "we" do they mean "we Americans" or "we Christians," because those are not the same. The role of the church and the role of the state, in the US, are distinct and unlike the theocracy of ancient Israel. Here are some sentences that show examples of the category mistake:

> "We should care for the poor." Do you mean "we" Christians or "we" the secular American government?

> "We should help immigrants." Do you mean "we" believers or "we" the US border patrol?

> "We should go kill the terrorists." Do you mean "we" churchgoers or "we" the US military?

Christians often commit this fallacy in theology when they describe God. If you think that God literally changes his mind, for example, you have committed this fallacy. Remember, all our language about God, as Aquinas would say, is analogical. God is a being wholly other than us. He is infinite, Trinity, simple, omnipresent, omnipotent, eternal, invisible, immutable, etc. He is *qualitatively* different from us. He is not higher up on the scale; he is on an entirely different scale.

When we say God is "big," that is fine if we are just trying to get the concept of his power across to a little kid. But, technically, God is not big because God is outside the dimensions of space and time. The designators *big* and *small* do not literally apply to God. To think of him as a spatial being is to commit a category mistake.

Calling abortion a "woman's body issue" is, not only a terrible equivocation, but a category mistake as well. It attempts to take the issue of infanticide and hide it under the banner of women's health. So anytime you attempt to protect a baby from being sucked out with a medical vacuum, someone can instantly change the category and say that you actually hate all women (except, of course, for the little woman, inside the bigger woman, who you are trying to keep alive). But all this is one big logical fallacy. Abortion has never been a woman's body issue. The baby is not the woman's body just because it is *inside* the woman's body any more than you are a ship just because you go on a cruise. The baby is completely different from the mother. It has its own, distinct DNA, its own fingerprints, its own heartbeat, its own brain, its own dreams, its own body, and, if you are a Christian, its own soul. Behind the murder of millions of babies stands the stupid logical fallacy of a category mistake.

Some churches will not allow a single guy to be a pastor because 1 Timothy 3 and Titus 1 say that he must be the "husband of one wife." That is a category mistake. *The text is not saying he must have a wife; it is saying, if he does have a wife, he can have only one.* Jesus was single. Paul was single. Almost all pastors for 1,500 years of church history were single. Paul says being single makes you *better* at ministry because you can spend more time focused on it (1 Cor. 7:32–35). If you want to take the text to say that you *must* be married, then in addition to being married, you also have to have multiple children (because the text mentions "children"), and your kids would have to still be young (the text mentions they are still under your authority), etc. This position is a category mistake. The text is assuming that *if* you are married, your marriage should look like this (only one spouse). The text is assuming that *if* you have kids, your children should look like this (obedient). It is not saying you must be married or have kids.

Here is another fallacy that comes from the long ending of Mark 16:9–20. Now, it is helpful to note that most scholars do not believe that this section is original to Mark (which is why almost all Bible versions have brackets around it). But we don't have time to get into textual criticism here. Mark 16:16 says, "Whoever believes and is baptized will be saved, but whoever does not believe will be condemned." I've heard people use this verse to say that water baptism is absolutely necessary for salvation. Now, forget the fact that this passage is not original to Mark; this type of reasoning commits the category mistake fallacy. This passage makes only two claims:

1. If someone believes and is baptized, then they will be saved.
2. If someone does not believe, they will be condemned.

Notice that the text says absolutely nothing about what happens to the person who believes but dies before they get a chance to get baptized. Those people would still be saved. Belief is the essential element, not baptism (which is why lack of belief is the only thing listed that condemns the person).

Hasty Generalization

This fallacy is described pretty clearly by its name. A hasty generalization means that you . . . generalize hastily! That is, you take information about something and quickly rush to a grand conclusion.

For example, let's say you are visiting the city of Miami and you come across several people who like their local football team, the Miami Dolphins. After you meet five Dolphins fans you might conclude, "Everyone in the city of Miami is a Miami Dolphins fan." But you have moved too quickly. There exists, in Miami, at least someone who is not a Miami Dolphins fan. Perhaps they like the Dallas Cowboys, the New York Giants, or even the Cleveland Browns.

You have to be aware of this fallacy when you see the words *all* or *none*.

"All Baptists think it is wrong to dance," is a hasty generalization. "All Presbyterians hate raising their hands in worship," is a hasty generalization. The statements "All Republicans love guns" and "All Democrats care about the poor" both commit this fallacy.

This error occurs in our churches regarding *adiaphora* issues. The term *adiaphora* refers to issues that are morally neutral; they are matters of conscience. An adiaphora issue is something that the Bible does not command but also does not forbid. Things like drinking, dancing, tattoos, playing cards, eating meat, owning a gun, watching movies, and getting cosmetic plastic surgery fall under this category.[4] However, because (like all good things) people can use them sinfully, we sometimes assume that all drinking is bad or all dancing is bad or all movies are bad. Those are hasty generalizations.

What is often needed is nuance. As we learned in Chapter 7, the way you refute a universal claim (all or none) is with just one example. The hasty generalization fallacy ignores the exceptions to these claims.

Misapplying a Situation

We won't spend a lot of time on this fallacy because it is simply when someone misreads a particular situation. They take some components of one situation and errantly read them onto a different situation without noticing the differences between the two.

I'll give you a few examples from the Bible. Several times, the Bible commands us to "greet one another with a holy kiss." Does this mean that you are sinning if you don't kiss everyone at your church door? Think about all the weirdos who would like to join your church's welcome team if you did! That would be misapplying the situation. The command, at its core, is to greet one another warmly—like brothers and sisters. The specific cultural context in the first century is a kiss, but today that same sentiment is expressed with a handshake or a hug. If you thought the text was saying you literally had to mouth-kiss everyone in your congregation, that would cause, not unity, but division. It would be misapplying the situation.

I once heard a couple quote Proverbs 21:9, "It is better to live in a corner of the housetop than in a house shared with a quarrelsome wife," as justification for why they thought they should get divorced. Notice the text doesn't say that a quarrelsome wife is grounds for divorce. It just says how awful a nagging wife can be. To use this text for divorce is to misapply the situation.

I've heard people mention how Deborah was an Old Testament judge or how Phoebe is called a "deacon," and then jump to the strange conclusion that women should therefore be elders of a local church. Now, this does not mean I think that women should or should not be in church leadership. This is not a theology book. It is simply to say that, regardless of your position, this line of reasoning is flawed. Deborah's temporary role as a political leader in Israel or Phoebe helping the church as a servant has nothing to do with what we have thought regarding the issue of female pastors throughout church history.

I've heard people say that it is hypocritical to kill people who are murderers because you are condemning their killing with more killing. This is misapplying the situation (and it is also an equivocation). *The just taking of life by the state is different from the unjust taking of life by an individual.*

In all these issues a situation is being misapplied. Before you can read one situation onto another, you have to see what is similar and what is different in the two situations.

False Cause *(post hoc ergo propter hoc)*

I would encourage you to check out "Chapter 9: Causation" to better understand this fallacy. There are a lot of errors in thinking when people talk about "cause." I have heard people say that "my wife caused me to cheat on her." What exactly does this mean? Does it mean she physically pushed you into another woman's bed? Or are you just trying to excuse your sin because your marriage was tough? Using the word *cause* is tricky and most people misunderstand it.

When it comes to politics, I've heard someone say that we should vote for pro-choice candidates (who are good on other economic issues) "because fewer people will have to commit abortions if other facets of the economy are doing well." I'm sorry . . . *have to* commit abortions? Regardless of who is elected to office, nobody is *making* anyone commit abortions. That is not how causation works. This argument is a logical fallacy.

But there is a specific causation fallacy that is quite common called a *"post hoc ergo propter hoc."* In Latin this means "after this, therefore because of this." It is the idea that just because one thing follows another in time, the first thing *caused* the second thing.

An example of this fallacy is when someone says, "A child played violent video games and then shot someone at their school;

therefore, the video games *caused* the child to be violent." Just because some angry teenager decided to commit a mass shooting that doesn't mean video games *made* him do that. What about all the kids who play violent video games and don't shoot up schools? How about all the children who seek out violent video games because they are *already violent* or because they have an abusive father?

Or you might have heard someone say that if you play classical music to your children when they are little, they will grow up to be smarter. Is that because the classical music strongly affects the little brains of those children, or is it because *they have the kind of parents who care for them so much that they are even thinking about what music they listen to when they are infants?*

One of the biggest fights I ever got into with my wife (and I know this sounds super stupid) is regarding something called "restless leg syndrome." Restless leg syndrome is a condition in which someone is continually moving their legs because they just can't get comfortable. Here was my question: "Does restless leg syndrome cause your legs to hurt, or do your legs hurt and you call the resulting motion restless leg syndrome? Is restless leg syndrome something you can put in a vial like anthrax or small pox? Is it something that is contagious? Is it an actual substance or *is it just a term we use to describe 'legs-that-are-not-comfortable' without actually naming the real cause of the discomfort?"* Or consider someone who said, "My alcoholism caused me to get drunk." That seems like a strange sentence. Did the repeated drunkenness cause the alcoholism, or did the alcoholism cause the repeated drunkenness? Oftentimes, we give a name to something (when we don't know what it is) and then, because we gave it a name, we act like it is a newly existing substance—a newly existing thing or diagnosis.

Pretend that as I go to open my refrigerator, someone rings my doorbell. Later, I go to open my refrigerator again and, by chance, someone else rings my doorbell. I might assume that opening my refrigerator is *causing* the doorbell to ring. But that is silly. Just because something follows something else in time that doesn't mean it is being *caused* by that thing.

This fallacy is found in the error of baptismal regeneration, which is the idea that the water ritual known as "baptism" *causes* one to be regenerated by the Spirit. But that is a *post hoc* fallacy. Just because the ritual of baptism is often seen around the same time that someone is converted in the New Testament, that doesn't mean the baptism *caused* the conversion. One is saved by grace alone through faith alone. Just because baptism happens around the same time one is saved doesn't mean that water is *causing* the salvation. In Acts 10 there is even the clear example of Cornelius's household being born again and regenerated *before* being baptized.

Bottom Line: Know what you mean when you use words like *caused* and *have to.* Furthermore, know that just because something follows something else in time, that doesn't necessarily mean it was caused by the previous thing.

Slippery Slope

In 1985 a book called *If You Give a Mouse a Cookie* was released. In the story, a mouse wants a cookie. But when you give the mouse a cookie, he wants some milk to go with it. When you give him milk, he wants a straw to drink the milk. And the mouse continues to want other things, which creates a snowball effect—all because you gave him a cookie.

One might reason that "since the mouse will always want more, you should not give him a cookie." But that way of thinking might turn into the fallacy of a slippery slope. Maybe you just give the mouse a cookie and tell him no when he asks for milk. Whoever keeps giving in to the mouse's tyrannical demands seems to be a bit of a pushover.

With the slippery slope fallacy, one argues for or against a position based on some extreme to which the position could be pressed. It assumes that because some position *could* be taken to an extreme, it *necessarily will* be taken to that extreme.

People often commit the slippery slope fallacy when they want to pull the reigns on grace. They say something like, "If we teach people about grace and about the security of their salvation, then they will run into deplorable sin." That type of thinking is a slippery slope.

Abuse does not negate proper use. Martin Luther once said:

> Do you suppose that abuses are eliminated by destroying the object which is abused? Men can go wrong with wine and women. Shall we then prohibit and abolish women? The sun, the moon, and the stars have been worshipped. Shall we then pluck them out of the sky?[5]

We have a tendency to want to argue against something because it could be taken to some extreme position. But that's not right. We should deal with the issue being made and not some hypothetical extreme view of the situation.

Regardless of what you think about the doctrine of predestination, it is not true that, if people believe in unconditional election, they will not evangelize. The entire first Great Awakening (and the fact that many of the fastest growing churches in the US are Calvinistic) shows that type of reasoning to be flawed.

However, slippery slope–style thinking is not always wrong. It all depends on whether someone's position is likely to lead to an extreme. For example, when gay marriage became legal in the United States, there were those who said that it would become a slippery slope. Without a fixed and standard definition of legal marriage, the door would be open to people wanting to define marriage in all types of ways. The LGBTQ community said that was a slippery slope argument that should be dismissed. But within the same year that gay marriage was declared legal, many other types of nontraditional marriage groups pushed to have their unions legalized. This use of the argument wasn't a fallacy, it was more like a prophecy.

So, do we have to take into account what people will do with particular issues when we are thinking about a slippery slope? You bet. But does that invalidate an argument just because people can take it to strange extremes? It does not.

Strawman Fallacy

With the strawman fallacy, instead of critiquing the actual position of your opponent, you create a weaker version of their argument (a caricature), so you can easily knock it over . . . like a scarecrow.

This fallacy is almost always used by someone's opponents. Those who like guns are called "crazed gunmen who want everyone to own nukes" and those who oppose guns are called "crazed hippies who want to eliminate self-defense and become slaves of the government." Calvinists and Arminians do this to each other. The Calvinists accuse the Arminians of not believing in God's sovereignty, and the Arminians accuse the Calvinist of being robots.

Some people support their own arguments with strawmen. Let's look at the debate between credo and paedo (infant) baptism.

Credo-baptism refers to the belief that only someone who has personally believed in Christ should be baptized. Paedo-baptism refers to the belief that children (who are too young to believe) should be baptized into the covenant people of God. One cannot prove believer's baptism just by showing how baptism is done in the New Testament; the argument is much more complicated than that (it includes how the covenants go together, the nature of the church, what the New Covenant promises are in Jeremiah and Ezekiel, etc.). Conversely, the person who believes in infant baptism cannot appeal to its similarity to circumcision (the candidates for New Covenant signs are different, the definition of "family" changes in the New Testament, and New Covenant promises are different from the Abrahamic Covenant). One also cannot look to passages that say entire families are being baptized (as the text doesn't mention the age of the family members). Each side should try to understand the other side. Both sides can't be right. But neither side is stupid. Each side must avoid the strawman fallacy and present the best argument they can for their position (as well as going after the best arguments made by their opponents).

I remember wanting to study atheism at one point in college. I wanted to know the best arguments for it. So, I emailed one of the top atheistic scholars in the US to ask what books I should read. He recommended his own books (as atheists tend not to be very humble), so I would have the strongest arguments that could be made for atheism. We should not be afraid of the truth. Atheism is wrong, but you cannot use a strawman argument by just saying things like, "If evolution is true then why are there still monkeys?" You can't just critique weak arguments and then claim victory. If you really want to engage with atheistic thought, you have to read Hume, Sartre, Camus, and Nietzsche. You can't settle for the sophomoric and embarrassingly ignorant writings of many modern atheists like Richard Dawkins, Sam Harris, or Daniel Dennett. Read the best positions against what you believe, not just the people who already agree with you.

Believe it or not, there are usually good arguments, even for silly positions, and those arguments have to be addressed.

Red Herring

This fallacy has an interesting name; it refers to a fallacy in which one tries to throw someone (or the audience) off the trail of an argument by distracting them with another issue. Someone once told me that the name of this fallacy comes from the practice of training dogs to sniff things out. In training dogs to follow certain scents, the trainers would use fish (usually, herring) to try to distract the dogs and throw them off the trail. Hence the name, "red herring."

This fallacy is pretty easy to spot. Instead of responding to the issue, someone will try to distract from the issue at hand.

Imagine that your church is having a meeting to discuss building a larger facility. You believe that your church doesn't have the money to do it. Additionally, you believe that it might be better to plant more churches instead of creating one giant monstrosity of a campus. You stand and explain why your church should not take on this additional debt and build a larger building. Your opponent then gets up and, instead of dealing with your argument, starts talking about how many lost people there are in your city and how you don't trust God enough to provide the money for the building. They may be able, by their rhetoric, to persuade the church to build a bigger building, despite the fact that they haven't actually made a case for it. In doing so, they use something Christians are passionate about (saving the lost) as a red herring, or a distraction, to disregard the information you gave. So, what began as a debate about church resources becomes a debate about whether you want lost people to go to hell and whether you trust God.

Or imagine that two Christians are debating about whether the sign gifts (tongues, prophesy, etc.) exist today. One person begins by giving reasons why they don't think those gifts are around today, and the other one says, "Don't you think that God has the power to raise someone from the dead?" Well, that wasn't the question, was it? Was the debate about what God *can* do or what God *does* seem to do throughout church history? Or, to critique the debate the other way, imagine that you are making a biblical case for why the sign gifts are around today and your opponent says, "Oh, so you think God wants us to just go crazy in church?" Is that really what you were arguing for? Or is that a red herring used to distract from your argument?

Bottom Line: Watch out for people who try to distract from the main argument with something else that our minds readily want to follow.

Poisoning the Well

Imagine living back in ye old days when you had to get your drinking water out of a well. But one day, people in your village start getting sick. It is determined that someone has poisoned the well. Knowing this, are you going to still use that well? Are you going to just use a little bit of the water and hope that some of it hasn't been infected by the poison? No way! You are going to stay away from it and get your water from some other source.

In this fallacy, one person tries to taint everything associated with a particular person, party, group, or topic. Instead of dealing with the argument, they try to make a particular category repulsive to anyone who would want to draw from it.

You see this in politics all the time. People will do the best they can to make a politician seem awful (through the news, social media, etc.). That way they can dismiss even true claims or good policies that politician has because the well has already been poisoned. Anyone associated with that politician is now seen as crazy. If you simply stand up in a crowd and say what political party you belong to, you will instantly be judged based on how culture has divided the political landscape.

I've heard pastors dismiss good things other pastors have to say because they are of a different denomination. I've heard pastors say that all complementarians are chauvinists or that all egalitarians are heretics. I've heard many Protestant pastors reject some idea as "Catholic" despite the fact that if you are a Protestant, about 90 percent of what you believe has already been held by the Roman Catholic Church! To reject everything "Catholic" would mean that you would have to reject the Trinity, the hypostatic union, the resurrection, etc.

Right now, this fallacy is being used against entire groups of people. If you are a white male, you are seen as a bad guy due to two factors you cannot change: your biological sex and your race. If you are an authority figure such as a police officer, you are instantly seen as a racist (even if you are a black police officer). Both of these are examples of poisoning the well. People who don't like stereotypes get society to stereotype other people so that culture won't listen to them. That is poisoning the well.

This fallacy is easy to spot. It happens when someone is trying to make a much larger category look bad instead of dealing with the specific issue at hand.

Moving the Goalposts

When you prove your claim or disprove your opponent's claim, they move the boundary line (the goalposts) further back, so they don't have to admit defeat.

I'll give you an example. I remember talking to a guy who was an atheist a while back, and we were talking about the traditional "proofs" for the existence of God. I was able to back him into a corner where he had to admit that the universe cannot be eternal going backward (or else how would we have gotten to today?), and that whatever started the universe cannot be material. He then said, "Yeah, but that doesn't prove that it's the *God of Christianity* who exists."

That is the fallacy of moving the goalposts.

We were not debating *which* God exists. We were debating whether any God exists. There are other reasons why I think it is specifically the *Christian* God who exists. But that wasn't the debate. The debate was whether the universe is eternal, and I had shown that it could not be. The man wanted me to prove that some God exists (and I did). Then, since he didn't like the outcome, he "moved the goalposts" so that I would have to meet another criteria before he would change his mind. *The proof we discussed didn't mean that he had to become a Christian, but it did mean that he couldn't be an atheist anymore.*

I've seen this conversation happen many times before:

> Non-Christian: "I don't believe the Bible because I found a contradiction in one of the passages."
>
> Pastor: (Explains why it is not actually a contradiction).
>
> Non-Christian: "Well, but the Bible wasn't written in English."

Pastor: "Yes, but I know Hebrew and Greek, and it says the same thing there."

Non-Christian: "Oh yeah, then why are there so many Bible translations?"

Pastor: "Because there are different methods of interpretation, but none of the translations contain what you claim to be a contradiction."

Non-Christian: "Oh yeah, but what about extra books that were not included in the New Testament?"

Pastor: "They were not included because they are not authentic. They were not written by the Apostles (or someone who knew an Apostle), they were written way too late to be authentic, they contain errors, and they were never accepted by God's people."

Non-Christian: "Oh yeah . . ."

And the conversation just keeps going. No matter how well the pastor answers skeptics' questions, they keep "moving the goalposts" back so the pastor doesn't score a goal.

Basically, this fallacy happens when a person doesn't allow an argument to win because, no matter what evidence is given for the argument, they can always create another hurdle that one has to jump over.

To give a more common example, the LGBTQ movement claims that one cannot change their sexual orientation. However, there are gay men who have become Christians and claim that they are now attracted to women. This evidence disproves that one cannot change their sexual orientation. However, since that is detrimental to the claim that you cannot change your orientation, the LGBTQ movement will move the goalposts. They will say that the man was never really gay or that he isn't really attracted to women. Notice what is happening. Anytime there is evidence that defeats their position they just find a way to make it impossible for them to be wrong.

Or if someone were to say, "You are a racist." You might respond, "Why am I a racist? I don't think negatively of any other races." To which they retort, "The very fact that you can't see you're a racist shows how blind you are to this issue." There is no way to win an argument like this because there is no argument. This is just one example of a person moving the goalpost (in this case, the definition of *racism*) so that you cannot show them that they are being silly.

A great way to deal with this fallacy is to simply ask this question, "What evidence could I give you that would cause you to admit that you are wrong?" If they can't answer this question, then they are someone who probably loves moving the goalposts.

Appeal to Experience

This fallacy is becoming increasingly common in our postmodern culture. *Instead of dealing with an argument, someone appeals to their own personal experience.* This fallacy is really a veiled power play to gain control on an issue by appealing to one's experience (or demographic) instead of giving reasons for why one believes what they believe.

This next part is a little nerdy, but you need to understand existentialism to understand why this fallacy has become so popular.

For much of Western history, truth was seen as objective; that is, something's "essence" existed before your experience of it. Think of essence as a definition of what something is. Essence preceded existence. Things were true regardless of your experience of them; it was true even before you were born. Sharing was good regardless of what you thought about it. Adultery was bad regardless of what you thought about it. Marriage was defined as a union between a man and a woman regardless of what you thought about it. Your personal experience was shaped around truth, not the other way around. In existentialism the opposite is true. Truth begins with you. Your personal acquaintance with something (existence) precedes the truth about what something is objectively (essence). You define what things are; they don't come predefined. Existentialism begins with an emphasis on the human experience (including personal freedom, self-actualization, and the absurdity of life) over the focus on truth.

In existentialism, one's experience trumps truth.

Here are the types of sentences you hear from people who appeal to experience:

> "You can't speak truth to me because you are of a different race than me and don't know what I've been through."

> "Speaking truth in the wrong way makes it untrue."

> "I don't have to listen to what you say because I don't like the way you are saying it."

> "You just don't 'get it.'"

> "You just can't see this issue clearly because of your background."

You see this fallacy a lot when someone appeals to race, gender, marital status, socioeconomic standing, sexual orientation, or whether someone has been a victim as a way to not have to listen to an argument. Anytime someone ignores an argument or wants to shut down a conversation because they have a different experience than you, they have committed this subtle fallacy.

The irony of this fallacy is that it takes those who previously didn't have a voice and gives them a voice, *only by taking away the voice of others.* It allows a former victim to become a current victimizer.

You often see this fallacy when Christians debate whether spiritual gifts exist today. To prove that they either do or do not, you have to make a case from the Bible. All appeals to what one has experienced are irrelevant. You may have experienced what you believe to be speaking in tongues, but you still have to prove it from scripture. Conversely, you may think that speaking in tongues no longer happens. You also have to prove your case from scripture. Anecdotal evidence is irrelevant to what scripture says.

When someone says that "men don't have a right to comment on abortion because it is a 'woman's body issue,'" they commit the fallacy of appealing to experience (in addition to an equivocation). Whether abortion is the murder of a person who is a different human than the mother is not based on experience at all.

Imagine that you are married and that a single person comes up to you and begins giving you advice on your marriage. You might be inclined to think, "How on earth can this single guy tell me about marriage?" But that type of thinking is an appeal to experience. If what the single guy is telling you is biblical, you have to listen to it; if it is not biblical, you can reject it. His marital status has no relevance to whether he is right. After all, Jesus and Paul were single, and we get most of our marriage advice in the New Testament from them.

This fallacy is dripping with pride. It seeks to make one's experience, gender, race, socioeconomic level, etc. the ultimate standard of truth instead of the Bible. It seeks to disregard the views of anyone who is unlike the person committing the fallacy.

Appeal to Popular Opinion (*ad populum*)

This fallacy happens when one makes an argument simply by appealing to what a lot of people think is true.

So instead of proving that their case is right, a person simply shows that a lot of people *think* a particular position is right. When someone says, "Everybody thinks this way," or "Nobody agrees with you," they may be committing the *ad populum* fallacy.

Here is the main problem with this fallacy: *Whether something is true has absolutely nothing to do with whether people think that it is true.* The majority of people used to think that germs didn't exist. Germs did not cease to exist due to their opinions. If everyone thought that the sky was pink, that would not, in fact, make it pink.

You'll often see polls showing what the majority of Americans think about immigration or tax reform or whatever. There is nothing wrong with those statistics, in and of themselves, but sometimes, they are used as a form of the *ad populum* fallacy. In effect, the news outlet is saying, "A bunch of people think something is good or bad, so it must be good or bad."

Again, like most of these fallacies, there is a way to properly appeal to a group of people. For example, let's say I was talking to someone who denied the Trinity and I said to them, "Literally, all orthodox Christian groups have held to the doctrine of the Trinity. Therefore, it seems strange for you to think that you are the first one in church history to get 'who God really is' right." In that case I'm not committing the fallacy because I'm not saying that the *reason* they are wrong is because a lot of people disagree with them. I'm saying they are wrong because the Bible teaches that God is a Trinity, and simply appealing to others in church history is a way to get them to question their errant and novel position.

You might think that a pure democracy would be a good way to make decisions. After all, if you are an American, you probably want the views of all people properly represented. It may surprise you to know that throughout most of world history, many people have thought that democracy is a horrible idea! If the majority of people are somewhat politically ignorant, why would we want to make decisions by counting heads instead of weighing arguments? Do you really want the person with no education, who is a meth dealer, and who belongs to the KKK having the same political authority as someone who has a PhD in economics and public policy from Harvard? If most people are non-Christian and untrained in political theory (which is true), then why do we want those same people making the decisions for everyone? Now, don't get me wrong. There are ways to still give people the right to vote and mitigate chaos through constitutional rights, representatives, etc. We live in a democratic republic and that is certainly better than most other political systems (such as Communism). However, I wonder if we often associate the *right* view with the *most-voted-on* view. That is the *ad populum* fallacy.

Sometimes, the majority opinion is correct. But many times, the majority opinion is wrong.

Confusing Probability and Possibility

You have no idea how many times I've heard sermons in which a pastor says, "Well, the Greek word in this biblical text *can* mean (blank)." Let me be as clear as I can: I could not care less what a word *can* mean. I want to know what it means, and I want the pastor to prove it.

In this fallacy, a person confuses something that is merely possible with thinking that it is therefore probable. There are many things that are possible, but that doesn't mean they are most likely. It is possible that unicorns exist. It is possible that Hinduism is true. It is possible that you are in a dream right now. That doesn't mean that any of those things is likely.

This fallacy is notorious for cropping up in theology. Many people think that because different interpretations are *possible* that one is not more probable than another. Soul sleep is possible, but it is not probable. Purgatory is possible, but it is not probable.

Oftentimes, someone will argue against a biblical position because a text *can be* interpreted in a certain way. They act like the mere existence of another possibility means that they are both equally likely. That is the fallacy of confusing probability and possibility. Just because there are several options, that does not mean that they are all equally probable.

When you fly in an airplane, you have two options: living and dying. The plane could make it, or the plane could crash. Both options are possible. Does that mean that they are equally likely? Would you say that there is a 50/50 chance that you will die on an airplane because there are only two options? No. Your chance of dying in a plane crash is infinitesimally small. *Just because there are two possibilities, that does not mean they are equally probable.*

Every time you weigh a theological position, a political position, or a social position, they can all appear to be possible. But who cares about that? Ask yourself which one is most probable. Ask yourself, "Is the position I'm holding more probable than not?" or "Which position is 51 percent or more likely?"

The bottom line on this fallacy is that whenever someone gives multiple positions, you need to ask yourself: Which one is *most* likely? Which one has a higher chance of being right?

Loaded Question

Let me ask you a question, and you have to answer with either yes or no:

Have you stopped beating your wife?

You can easily see the problem with this fallacy. You cannot truly answer the question if you are not a wife-beater. If you say yes, you imply that you used to beat your wife. If you say no, you imply that you beat her currently.

Or if someone said to you, "Do you believe in macro-evolution, or are you someone who denies science?" In addition to being a false dichotomy, this question commits the loaded question fallacy. It assumes that if you don't believe in modern evolutionary theory, then you somehow are anti-truth or anti-science.

Or if someone said, "Do you believe that all the symbols in Revelation are literal, or do you not really believe God's word?" That is a loaded question. You can love the Bible and maintain nuanced views on how to interpret the book of Revelation.

A loaded question has a hidden premise in the question that you might not want to affirm, though the question takes it for granted. This is why you have to be careful when someone asks you to only answer yes or no. Sometimes, this is a way to hide a loaded question under the guise of being direct.

Here is what is so tricky about the loaded question fallacy: *It is very subtle.* Whenever someone asks you a question, they could be implying certain things in the question that you end up accidentally affirming just by engaging in the conversation.

Imagine that there is a Hispanic supremacy group that thinks Hispanics are the master race. Imagine that there is also an Asian supremacy group that thinks Asians are the master race (like the Japanese in WWII). These two groups clash at a local protest, and you are asked by a reporter, "Don't you condemn the actions of the Hispanic supremacy group?" Well, the short answer is yes (as Christians we should condemn all racial supremacy whether it be white, black, Asian, Hispanic, or anything else). However, because there are two sides to the story, the reporter might assume that if you say yes, you actually support the Asian supremacy group, and if you say no, the reporter might assume that you support Hispanic supremacy. In this hypothetical situation, a loaded question is preventing you from saying what you need to say, which is "I condemn both forms of racial supremacy." This happens often when two groups of protestors violently clash. Instead of condemning both sides for their violence, some people will only focus on one side (and thus appear to implicitly support the other side).

Or assume for a moment that someone asks you, "Don't you think it is awful when men sexually assault women?" The answer to that question is an unequivocal yes. But now let's assume that the question is being asked in the context of a court case in which a woman has *falsely* accused someone of sexual assault (when the sex was actually consensual). Now, what originally seemed to be a clear-cut question involves a loaded question so that to simply speak to one side of the issue means you (implicitly) support the other side. Christians must say the truth, the whole truth, and nothing but the truth. In this case we would say, "Sexual assault is always evil and sinful. This particular case was not a case of sexual assault, but rather a false allegation of sexual assault." Loaded questions try to prevent you from saying all that you need to say.

Loaded questions often appear on issues where there seem to only be two prevailing views. To say anything negative about one side is taken as an implication that you like the opposing side. When there are two bad sides to an issue, a loaded question will try to get you to just focus on one side.

Avoid falling into this logical trap.

Begging the Question (*petitio principii*)

Oftentimes, especially on the news, you will hear a reporter say, "This begs the question, what will the mayor do next?" or some sentence like that. What the reporter means to say is "This *leads to* the question." "Begging the question" does not mean "leads to the question," but is rather a *terminus technicus* for a logical fallacy.[6]

Begging the question means that you assume your conclusion in your premise. You assume the very thing that you are supposed to be proving. To say, "This man is stupid because . . . look how stupid he is," is arguing in a circle. It is begging the question.

You see this fallacy when you are talking to someone who believes the earth is flat. For any proof you put forward, they will say it didn't happen or isn't true. Why? Because they have already assumed what they are trying to prove, namely that the earth is flat. So, if you say, "What about the people who have been in space and seen that the earth is a sphere?" They may say, "We have never been to space," or "All the windows have been altered to make the earth look that way." Notice they didn't prove that we have never been to space; they have just begged the question. They assume that, because seeing the earth as spherical from space would be devastating to their argument, we have never really been there. Or if you say, "What about when two planes travel in different directions around the earth and get to the same location?" They may say, "That never actually happens," or "There is another explanation for that," or "That's just what the airline industry wants you to believe." Let me assure you that many people, myself included, have flown internationally, and you can get to one location traveling several different ways. If you say, "What about a ship that travels in one direction continually?" They will say, "The government will intercept the ship, so it doesn't keep traveling," or "The equipment on the ship is actually deceptive," or some other equally crazy sentence. Of course, that's just not true. Ships sail in one direction all the time, and they are not stopped by the government nor do they fall off the map (pun intended). In addition to using the fallacy of "moving the goalposts," flat-earthers beg the question at every turn.

I've heard people say that when Jesus turned water into wine, the "wine" was actually grape juice because (they believe) drinking alcohol is a sin. Notice the fallacy. It can't be real wine because they have already assumed drinking is a sin. So, they start with their conclusion before they have demonstrated it. Drinking must be sinful, in their mind, so they have to find a way to say that Jesus didn't really turn water into real wine. I think it would be much more logical to assume that drinking is not sinful because Jesus turned water into real wine. Forget the fact that grape juice wasn't a thing until the pasteurization process was invented in 1864. Forget the fact that the Bible commands us not to get drunk with wine (*"oinos"* in Greek), which assumes it is alcoholic. Forget the fact that just about all Christians throughout church history used real wine in communion and didn't think drinking was sinful. Forget the fact that Matthew 11:18–19 says Jesus came eating and drinking alcohol. Forget the fact that the early church used wine (which is why the Corinthians are getting drunk during communion in 1 Corinthians 11:21). For the teetotaler, the pre-arrived-at-conclusion is that drinking is sinful, so the Bible must be twisted to fit within an already defined conclusion. Regardless of what you think about drinking, you can see that they haven't allowed their reasoning to ferment long enough and have committed the fallacy of begging the question.

Abortion activists commit this same fallacy: To kill a baby in the womb and to think that this is okay because it is not a baby is the fallacy of begging the question. They haven't proven that it is not a baby (with its own heartbeat, DNA, dreams, mind, fingerprints, etc.). Instead, they have just begun with their unproved assumption. Why do they believe it is not really a baby? *Because they don't want the fact that the baby is a little human to contradict the very conclusion with which they started.* Now, they might respond by saying, "No, Zach, we don't think that abortion is murder because the baby *is not viable apart from the mother.*" To which I would respond, "Why do you think 'viability-apart-from-the-mother' is the definition of what is and is not murder?" That is also begging the question. You see, they continue to argue in a circle and beg the question because, no matter where the truth would lead, they are unwilling to turn from their view. They start with their view that abortion is not murder, so every time you show them it is murder, they just go back to their (unproved) presupposition.

Begging the question is not always a logical fallacy. What do I mean? Well, anytime you make an appeal to an *ultimate* authority, you cannot appeal beyond that thing and must, therefore, appeal to it. That sounds really technical, so let me explain what I mean. If I want to prove that the Bible is true, I cannot appeal to anything higher than the Bible for my ultimate authority. If I appeal to a history book or a science book or my intellect or anything else, I have placed something above the authority of the

Bible. But this isn't just a problem for Christians. *All appeals to ultimate authority have to appeal to themselves.* Science appeals to the scientific method; it can't appeal beyond it. Math appeals to mathematical proofs; it can't appeal beyond it. Logic stands or falls on seemingly obvious rules like the law of non-contradiction. Every appeal to an ultimate authority is circular. It's only a fallacy *if you're wrong*—if you've chosen the wrong starting point.

In summary, this fallacy occurs when you assume something you are supposed to be proving.

Argument from Silence

Let me ask you this question: Biblically, who can pass out the elements for communion? The short answer is that the Bible doesn't tell us. Presumably, the pastor is the one presiding over communion, but the text doesn't say that the elements must be passed out by deacons or staff or men or women (or any other qualifiers). To hold a strong stance that only certain people can pass out communion is an argument from silence.

An argument from silence puts forward an argument that neither proves nor disproves their argument. It is an argument from silence. Silence doesn't make a very good argument because *silence doesn't say anything.*

Let me give you a phrase you will hear people misuse a lot in the church. When talking about some topic, people will ask, "Where is *that* in the Bible?" Well, that question might be a veiled form of the argument from silence fallacy. *Notice that something not being in the Bible is not the same as it being unbiblical.* Cars are not in the Bible. Air-conditioning is not in the Bible; iPhones are not in the Bible. That doesn't make these things unbiblical. People often assume because something is not explicitly mentioned in the Bible, it must therefore be bad. But that's not right. If I say, two plus two equals four and someone says, "Where is that in the Bible?" they have made an argument from silence. The Bible not saying something about an issue is not the same as condemning an issue. This is true regarding the debate between infant's and believer's baptism in the book of Acts. People will often point out that entire households are said to be baptized as evidence that the early church practiced infant baptism. But this is an argument from silence. *We don't know the ages of those in the household*, so this cannot be used to either support or deny infant baptism. If those in the household are old enough to believe, then the credobaptists have ammo for their position. If those in the household are infants, then the paedobaptists have ammo for their position. But because we don't know the ages, it is an argument from silence, and we have to evaluate other (clearer) passages to know who should be baptized.

Speaking of ammo. If an educator said, "We didn't have any school shootings in our school district this year, and that is because our schools do not allow guns on campus," that is an argument from silence. Maybe you just got lucky. Maybe a student brought a gun to school and decided not to use it. Maybe you live in a safe, wealthy area of town. Maybe you have police on campus to deter an active shooter. Maybe you allow teachers to carry concealed as a deterrent from violence. You see, it is an argument from silence to assume something that you cannot directly back up.

Middle Ground

In this fallacy a person states that the truth regarding two opposing views must be something in the "middle."

If you say the answer is 1 and I say the answer is 10, the middle ground fallacy is that the answer must be 5.

But is that true?

Let's say two people are arguing about whether adultery is wrong. One person says it is, and another says it is not. Is the truth that it is sometimes wrong but not at other times? I'd contend that it is always wrong.

Or let's say an atheist and a theist are debating whether God exists. Is the truth in the middle? It logically can't be in the middle because these two options are mutually exclusive.

You see, this fallacy is often used by someone who doesn't like conflict and wants to act like, "We can both be right." *Just because there are smart people on both sides of an argument doesn't mean that the arguments presented by both sides are equally smart.* There are smart Christians, and there are smart Muslims, but that doesn't mean that Islam is true or that some halfway point between the two positions is right.

I hear this language a lot in the conflict between Arminianism and Calvinism. People will argue that the truth must be somewhere in the middle. However, they are mutually exclusive positions. The five points of Calvinism are logically at odds with the five points given by the Remonstrants.

Sometimes, the truth between two positions is actually in the middle. Should one *never* eat sweets or *only* eat sweets? I think you should *sometimes* eat sweets. But the middle ground fallacy happens when one ignores arguments and instantly jumps to the middle of two positions.

Shifting the Burden of Proof

I've heard that in Scotland, when a jury returns to give its verdict on a criminal case, they don't say that the defendant is "guilty" or "not guilty" (like we do in the US). Rather, they return with a verdict of either "guilty" or "not proven." I think that is brilliant, and I don't know why we don't adopt this language in the US. The reason they don't use the not-guilty verdict is because the role of a jury in a criminal case is *not to determine someone's guilt; it is to determine whether a prosecutor has proven his case beyond a reasonable doubt.* The defendant may be as guilty as sin itself. But that's not how juries work. The defendant is innocent until proven guilty. *The burden of proof is on the prosecutor, not on the defendant.* If he is innocent or the prosecutor cannot make a very good case then, by default, he goes free.

Oftentimes, people will shift the burden of proof in an argument, and that is a logical fallacy.

It is the job of the person who is making the case to support their position; it is not the job of the person listening to disprove the case. We should not assume some position has been supported just because someone hasn't "shot it down" yet.

Imagine if someone proclaimed that "unicorns exist!" Now, let's be clear what we mean by unicorns. I don't mean some weird deer that accidentally grew a horn on its head that was discovered somewhere in the woods in Europe. I don't mean a goat that has one horn. I mean an actual, magic, flying, rainbow-colored, sparkly-horned unicorn. But suppose that when I ask why they think unicorns exist, the person said, "Well, you can't prove that they *don't* exist." With that response, they would have shifted the burden of proof. It is not my job to prove that unicorns don't exist. That is the standard, default view. It is the job of the one making the claim to prove that unicorns do exist. The burden of proof is on them.

This fallacy is often committed when people try to forbid something the Bible allows. They will ask, "Where does the Bible allow X?" Well, that is shifting the burden of proof. It is their job to show where the Bible forbids X, not my job to show where it allows X. If the Bible does not forbid it (either explicitly or by logical implication), then it is allowed. I don't have to prove that the Bible says I can drive a car (if, in some strange world they thought that was wrong for some reason). That is implied. If someone thinks driving a car is bad, they have to prove it. The burden of proof is on them.

I'm a big fan of church history. Why? Because it helps us best interpret the Bible. If someone comes up with some theological view that basically nobody (Catholic, Protestant, or Greek Orthodox) has ever held in over 2,000 years of church history, the chances are that they are probably wrong. They might be right; it is possible. But the burden of proof is on them to show how millions of Spirit-filled, Jesus-loving Christians (many of whom are way smarter than you or me) missed it. The burden of proof is not on the default, standard view of Christianity. The burden is on them to show why everyone in church history missed it. And their case better be pretty good if they are claiming that they got it right when Augustine, Anselm, Aquinas, Luther, Calvin, and Edwards all missed it.

One more thing on this fallacy. Sometimes, people will commit this fallacy by saying, "I'm not convinced yet" or "I'm not convinced by that argument." Usually, what they have done is to shift the burden of proof. In effect, they are saying that they don't have to support their argument; it just gets to be the default, and you are the only one who has to support your position. But they shouldn't get to just remain where they are because they are not "convinced." *They have to also put forward a more likely and more convincing argument than the one you used.* Always be cautious with "I'm not convinced" language. It's not always wrong, but it is often a subtle way for someone to shift the burden of proof.

Sometimes, people do this with questions and hypotheticals as well. They will ask a question or put forward a hypothetical situation and ask you to shoot holes in it. But this is the fallacy of shifting the burden of proof. Their question or hypothetical serves as a veiled form of a proposition and, instead of proving it, they instantly jumped to see whether you could poke holes in it. But you don't have to poke holes in it until they have put forward a reason for why they are asking the question or giving the hypothetical in the first place.

Let me give an example:

> Business executive: What would it look like if we sold all our product online instead of in the store?

> Employee: Well, that would be a problem because (insert business reasons here).

> Business executive: I don't agree with all those reasons, so let's move forward with selling all our product online.

Do you see what happened there? At no point did the executive give a reason for why it would be better to not sell any product in the store. His "question" was a Trojan horse. He put all the pressure (and the burden of proof) on the employee when it was not that employee's burden to bear.

Special Pleading

Imagine that I said, "No Scotsman (i.e., someone from Scotland) will turn down a chance to go to a rugby game." Now, an Englishman comes up and says, "That's not true; my friend John is from Scotland, and he hates rugby." And I reply, "Well, no *true* Scotsman will turn down a chance to go to a rugby game."

Do you see the fallacy I've committed? I've committed the fallacy of special pleading. This fallacy is, as you can see above, also called the . . . drumroll . . . "no true Scotsman" fallacy!

I made a claim that pertained to "all" people within a particular class (Scotsmen), but when I was shown to be wrong, I just adapted my position to say that anything that didn't agree with me didn't really fit within that class. That way, I didn't have to admit that I was wrong. That is the special pleading fallacy. When confronted about the Scotsman named "John," I should have just said, "You're right, *most* Scotsmen will not turn down a chance to go to a rugby game." This fallacy typically happens when a person makes a universal claim, and someone shows them an exception. Instead of accepting the exception, they just try to wiggle around it and plead a special case for that exception.

This happens a lot when someone changes their original argument because they see that their opponent is beating them intellectually.

When a psychic claims to know something about you, and they get it wrong, they might say that they are just having an off day or that your lack of belief is hindering their powers. That is special pleading. The real reason it doesn't work is because being a psychic is bogus; they are using the fallacy of special pleading to continue their money-making scam.

You see this fallacy in the televangelism world a lot. When a "faith healer" comes on TV, they often claim that "if you have enough faith," God will heal you of your disease (and healing is 100 percent guaranteed). So, what happens when you pray and have faith but are not healed? Well, they will say that you didn't have enough faith. Womp womp. That is special pleading. When their sovereignty-of-God-denying scheme is shown to be false, they just make a special case for why you didn't really have enough faith, which they always define as how *hard* you believe something. This is also an equivocation on the Bible's use of the word *faith*. If they really had a gift of healing, would it only work in some cases? If I have a gift of teaching or hospitality, does that only work if everyone in the room has enough faith, or is it pretty consistent? You see, for the televangelist trying to make money off you, the problem is not in their unsound view about biblical healing; the problem is actually you. You are just not good enough at conjuring up feelings of trust in God to heal you.

Be careful when someone makes a claim *and then tries to adapt it* after you have shown them to be wrong.

Logical Inconsistency

When you hold two positions and they contradict each other, at least one of the positions you hold is incorrect (see "Chapter 3: The Laws of Logic").

Let's look at two controversial examples mentioned by lobbyist and professor Ryan Anderson. These are issues with which the LGBTQ community is currently wrestling. The first regards how homosexuality and transgenderism are logically inconsistent and the second regards how feminism and transgenderism are logically inconsistent.[7]

If one affirms that (1) someone cannot change their sexual orientation but (2) they can change their gender, they have committed this logical fallacy.

Homosexuality and transgenderism are logically inconsistent with each other. If you hold to one view, you cannot hold to the other. What do I mean by this? Well, let me give you an example. Let's say that two men, Nathan and Jim, are in a same-sex relationship. They would claim that they were born that way and that they could not be sexually attracted to women. Now let's say that one of the men (Nathan) transitions into being a transgender woman and, though he was born with XY chromosomes and testicles, he believes that in reality, he is a woman. Furthermore,

Nathan decides not to make any physical changes to his body or tell Jim about his transition. This leads to one of two conclusions:

1. Jim is no longer gay because he is now in a sexual relationship with an actual woman.

   or

2. Nathan is not "really" a woman, and transgenderism has been shown to be false.

The first proposition offends the homosexual community (because it says you can change your sexual orientation), and the second proposition offends the transgender community (because it says you can't really change your gender). And yet, they must fight over it because they cannot both be true. If a gay man is attracted to someone who has become an *actual* woman then one's sexual orientation *can* change. If his partner can't really become an *actual* woman, then transgenderism is false. You can't have it both ways. The "LG" and the "T" in "LGBTQ" cannot go together logically speaking.

But the same logical inconsistency happens when someone claims to be a feminist and also support transgenderism. You can be one or you can be the other, but you cannot be both. Why not?

Imagine someone named "Jack" who lived as a man for 60 years. Jack doesn't know what it is like to be sexually objectified. Jack doesn't know what it is like to get paid less for the same job. Jack doesn't know what it is like to have his opinion dismissed, just because of his gender. Now let's say Jack transitions to become a transgender woman named "Jill." Can Jill really sympathize with the feminist cause?

Transgenderism conflicts with feminism because a man who claims to be a transgender woman now takes away any unique persecution that women have experienced because he can say he knows what it is like to be a woman when he actually doesn't. He can say he knows what it is like to be sexually objectified; he knows what it is like to not get paid equally in the workplace; he knows what it is like to have his opinion dismissed by men. But does he really? A man who transitions to become a woman robs women of everything that is unique to them. Feminism has traditionally claimed that men cannot speak to issues of abortion because they don't have a uterus or ovaries or female genitalia. Well, if a man claims to be a woman, then you either have to say that you don't need a uterus or ovaries or female genitalia to talk about abortion (thus, all men can speak to the issue), or you have to deny that those transgender persons are really the gender they claim to be. You can have one or the other, logically, but you cannot have both.

What if "Jill" is elected president? Does this mean that the US has really had its first female president? If you say yes, then you take away something that would have been unique to those born as biological women. If someone born as a biological woman then became president, she would only be the second female president in US history. If you say no, then you deny that someone can really change their gender.

Even using the term *transgender woman* shows that there is a difference in one's mind between that person and a real woman. If someone was really a woman, then they wouldn't use the term *transgender* at all. Ironically, the word *transgender* is transphobic.

When someone says, "You should not judge people," in addition to committing an equivocation (the Bible condemns *hypocritical* judging, not all judging of every type), they are also being logically inconsistent. They are judging the very person they are telling not to judge. They are contradicting themselves. They are trying to hold that (1) people should not tell other people they are wrong while (2) telling someone they are wrong.

Perhaps you have had a conversation with an older woman who thought that it was wrong for younger women to get their nose (or any other part of their body) pierced. Now, forget for a moment that women in the Bible have their noses pierced, and forget that this is even seen as an image of the blessing of God in selecting Israel (Ezek. 16:12, etc.). But these conversations go something like this:

> Older Woman: "I don't think women should be piercing their body."
>
> You: "But you have earrings. You have pierced your body twice."
>
> Older Woman: "Those are different. Piercing your ears is okay."
>
> You: "Why is it okay to pierce your ears but not other parts of your body? Where does the Bible parse out which parts of your body you can and can't pierce?
>
> Older Woman: "Well, I just don't like it."

You see, the older woman was not comfortable with her earrings because she had studied everything the Bible had to say about piercings. Rather, she just assumed that earrings are okay because they are accepted in her culture. She thought one kind of piercing that the Bible didn't condemn was okay but another type of piercing that the Bible didn't condemn was not. That is a logical inconsistency.

LOGICAL FALLACIES

One more thing to note. If you hold a position that is a logical contradiction to some position another person holds, at least one of you is wrong. But sometimes, both positions are wrong.

Imagine that someone says, "Chocolate ice cream is the best ice cream," and another person says, "Vanilla ice cream is the best ice cream." Now, they can't both be right. Both flavors cannot both be the "best." But, in this example, *both* people can be wrong. As we all know cookie dough and mint chocolate chip are far superior ice cream flavors to plain chocolate or vanilla. *So, in some cases, you cannot both be right, but you can both be wrong.*

But when there are only two options, and you contradict each other, you cannot both be right, *but you cannot both be wrong either.* Let me give you another example:

If you say, "God does not exist," and I say, "God does exist," we cannot both be right, and we cannot both be wrong. In cases where two positions are contradictions *and there are only two logical options,* then you cannot both be wrong either.

If someone is accusing you of being logically inconsistent, you can't ignore it as if it's just name-calling. They are pointing out that you are believing two things that logically contradict each other. This is a big deal! A logical contradiction means that at least one of the two things you are holding is wrong and/or sinful. The charge of "inconsistency" is the death blow to a philosopher.

Where are you being inconsistent in some of your beliefs?

The Composition Fallacy

"Everyone on the basketball team is a good player; therefore, the team is a good team." This is the fallacy of composition in which one assumes that a quality that applies to individuals also applies to the group.

141

It is true that, within the Catholic Church, there have been many cases of sexual assault. Sexual assault is evil, and anyone who has committed it, should not be protected by the church but must be turned over to the authorities for justice. It would be a fallacy, though, to think that, just because some priests have been pedophiles, every priest is. Many priests walk in total abstinence and would never think of hurting a child.

You sometimes see this fallacy when people recount bad things that "Christians" have done in the past. The Inquisition, the Crusades, and the wars by Spanish explorers against the people of South America were all promoted by people who claimed to be Christians. Now, forget the fact that when you don't follow the teachings of Christ, then you are not really a Christian. (Claiming to be a Christian and being a Christian are different.) But many people assume that because there were a few bad apples, then the whole tree is bad. That's not true and it also commits the composition fallacy. The same is true outside Christianity. We cannot assume that all atheists are mean or irrational just because many have been. We have to avoid the fallacy of composition every time it occurs.

The Division Fallacy

This is simply the opposite of the composition fallacy whereby people assume that a quality that applies to a group also applies to the individuals of that group. This fallacy would be something like, "The basketball team as a whole is good; therefore, every individual who plays on the basketball team is good." Really? What about the guy who rides the bench all year?

If I said, "This church seems trustworthy as a whole; therefore, you can trust every individual pastor at this church," I would be committing the division fallacy. There are some really awesome churches that have some really bad people on staff. What is true for the group (as a whole) is not true for everyone in that group.

You may also see this fallacy in politics. You might assume that, because a political party is supporting righteous policies, everyone in that party is righteous (which is surely not the case).

The bottom line for both of these fallacies (composition and division) is to avoid confusing the qualities of a larger group with those of the individual members of that group and vice versa.

Appeal to Force (*ad baculum*)

Imagine that you are Galileo and you are on trial for saying that the earth revolves around the sun. Instead of addressing your superior proofs from mathematics and astronomy, the church authorities ignore your arguments and simply tell you that if you do not recant you will be exiled, excommunicated, or executed.

That is an *ad baculum*. Instead of addressing an argument, someone makes a threat. The Latin word *baculum* used here is the word for *stick*. Roman authorities sometimes had a symbolic stick (almost like a scepter or a rod of authority) that was a symbol of their power to "strike" lawbreakers. That is where this fallacy derives its name. People often want to punish those who disagree with them instead of addressing their arguments.

Now, don't get me wrong. It is right to punish lawbreakers as such. But even before you can do that, *you have to have a trial where arguments are made for why they should be punished*. If you are Galileo (and if you are wrong), then it should be really easy to show you where you made a mistake in your calculations. People shouldn't just threaten you; they should be able to easily show you where your astronomy is off. If they cannot, maybe you are not as wrong as they are claiming.

This fallacy doesn't care about arguments. It simply tells you to change your mind . . . or else.

"If you hold that view, you will lose your job."

"You cannot believe that doctrine or else you will be fired."

"You better apologize right now, or I will never see you again."

"I'm going to punch you in the mouth."

These are all appeals to force.

Conversely, you have to continue to hold true positions even if you are threatened. The *ad baculum* is a fallacy for the person who makes it, *but it is also a fallacy for the person who gives into it*. If you are a Christian and turn against what the Bible teaches because of some threat (social pressure, name-calling, physical violence, imprisonment, getting fired, etc.), you have committed this fallacy as well. Don't be a coward. Be brave. Don't change your view because some less-logical person threatens you.

It is easier to demote, kill, imprison, silence, slander, criticize, ban, cancel, or harm someone than it is to show someone, who is right, that they are wrong.

Many people misunderstand this fallacy. It is not that all threats are wrong. *Threats when there are not reasons given are wrong*. But sometimes, a threat implies a reason for it even though it is not stated explicitly.

For example, if a police officer tells you to keep your hands out of your pockets or he will shoot you. That is not an *ad baculum*. He has a reason. The reason is that you may have a weapon in your pocket, and he doesn't have time to find out whether you want to kill him. He doesn't have time to say all that, but there is a (implied) reason and, therefore, it is not a fallacy.

When the Bible warns that those who do not know Christ will go to hell, that is not an *ad baculum* fallacy. Why? Because there is a reason for the command. You and I have sinned against an infinite being and, because he is just, he demands infinite punishment. There is a reason behind the command.

Suppose a teacher goes into a high school classroom and gives a lecture on why students should not have sex before they are married. The teacher says that the reasons they should not have sex are (1) they could get an STD and (2) they could get pregnant. Those statements are true, but are they the primary reasons students should not have sex before they are married? Is the ultimate reason for why high school students should not have sex because some inconvenient medical things might happen to them if they do?

That is an *ad baculum*. It makes an argument based solely on some bad thing that could happen (which are not the real reasons to wait until you are married). Biblically, the reason you should not have sex before you are married is because God condemns it as sin.

If I am a teenage boy in this scenario, I'm not hearing that fornication is bad; I'm only hearing that fornication is bad *if you do it the wrong way* (without protection). If I can have sex and not get an STD (and not get a girl pregnant), then I just learned that I'm free to go for it. Yes, avoiding premarital sex does lower your chances of getting an STD. But that's not the *main* reason to avoid it from a Christian worldview.

This is a pretty common fallacy. And if you don't believe me . . . I'll be mean to you!

You Too! (*tu quoque*)

"He pushed me," said one boy. "Well, that's just because he pushed me first," said the other boy. We have all heard arguments like this, especially growing up. In the *tu quoque* argument, someone points out a flaw in your position and, instead of addressing their argument, you show them some flaw in their position.

You don't get around the bad arguments in your position by trying to shift the argument back onto the other person. If a corrupt mayor, who was stealing money from the city, had a bank robber arrested for stealing money, the bank robber cannot try to defend themselves by saying, "But the mayor also stole money." It is true that he should point out that the mayor stole money, *but that just makes the mayor guilty; that doesn't make the bank robber innocent.*

To say it as simply as I can: *Two wrongs don't make a right.*

Trying to point out a flaw in someone or their position is totally fine. It is legitimate to point out bad arguments. But pointing out the fact that someone else is doing something wrong doesn't get rid of your bad arguments. *Their failure doesn't excuse your failure.* You have to first defend your position and address their objection. Only after that can you point out their flaws. You can point out bad arguments, but that mere "pointing-out" cannot be the actual case you are making for your argument.

This fallacy does not mean that you cannot point out flaws in people's arguments. *It means that you cannot point out flaws in people's arguments and try to act like your position has been defended as a result.*

Let's pretend I said to someone in church, "You misinterpreted this biblical passage" and then gave reasons for why their interpretation was wrong. They then respond with, "Well, my interpretation is correct because you misinterpreted the passage as well." Two wrong interpretations do not somehow make a right one. The *tu quoque* fallacy has been committed in this example.

You see this a lot in politics. Candidate A will say to Candidate B, "Your foreign policies got a lot of people killed unnecessarily." Instead of showing that this claim is false by using facts, Candidate B will respond, "Oh yeah, your economic policies led to a greater unemployment rate than we previously had." Notice how strange the *tu quoque* argument is. It shows only that two people have problems in their arguments, not that one doesn't have a problem just because the other person also has one.

Missing the Point *(ignoratio elenchi)*

This fallacy is similar to what is known as a *non sequitur*. A non sequitur means that a conclusion just straight-up doesn't follow from the argument being made. If I say, "We should invade Greenland because I had spaghetti last night," that is a non sequitur. However, in real life, the arguments are not as obvious as that (though they are sometimes just as ridiculous).

An *ignoratio elenchi* is a very similar fallacy, which is why I didn't include a separate category for non sequiturs. This fallacy occurs when one's argument goes off the rails by talking about something other than the point of the argument.

If a parent says, "We shouldn't watch that movie because it has too much nudity," and their teenager complains, "You never let me watch anything I want to watch," that teenager is committing this fallacy. They are missing the point. Whether a teenager feels as though their parents are letting them do what they "want" is irrelevant to why their parent's rule against watching nudity stands.

The book of Proverbs is very clear in saying that the way we should discipline our children includes corporal punishment—

what it calls the "rod." Despite what the Bible teaches about this issue (and what almost all humanity has believed about it), some parents say that physical discipline seems mean. That is an *ignoratio elenchi*. It misses the point. How something "seems" to our sinful, broken minds is different from whether it is something the Bible would have us do.

The statement that "women should serve in combat roles in the military so the military can be 'equal'" is an excellent example of this fallacy. To support the idea that you should have women in combat roles, you would have to prove that *it would improve all around combat effectiveness* and that standards would not be dropped. Any reason that pointed to an issue other than that (especially when one is seeking to promote some type of political social experiment) is an *ignoratio elenchi*.

You see this argument regarding global warming and climate change. Again, I'm not going to give my opinions on this issue one way or the other. Christians should balance taking care of the world God gave us with also using the world to our benefit. What I want to point out is that most people do not understand what the debate is actually about. The question is not, "Is the world getting warmer?" Some people debate that question, but it completely misses the point. The question is, "Can we know that human activity is making the world warmer considering we only have a few years of data?" And "Considering the US only makes up a very small percentage of the world's pollution, would any plan that we implemented work if the rest of the world was not on board?" Or "What solution wouldn't lead to the deaths of millions of humans caused by shutting down technology and industry?" Those are the better questions to discuss. The question has nothing to do with the world's temperature but with questions about the *cause and solution* to the world's temperature.

"We should do such-and-such in our church so we can increase our numbers or see more baptisms" is the same fallacy. If the great commission is to make full-blown disciples (and not half-baked converts), then this statement completely misses the point. The goal is faithfulness not pragmatism, worldly success, or "numbers."

Bottom Line: Avoid distracting arguments that do not deal with the actual issue at hand.

Appeal to Ignorance (*ad ignorantiam*)

This fallacy happens when someone appeals to the fact that their argument wasn't disproven (or we don't know the answer to the issue being debated) and then assumes that lack-of-knowledge somehow proves their argument.

If I say, "Unicorns exist," I am then obligated to prove that point. I cannot just say that someone else didn't do a good enough job of disproving unicorns, so therefore I'm right. I also cannot say, "There is not enough information about unicorns overall, so we should assume that my argument is right."

In this fallacy, ignorance is used as actual proof for your argument. As you can imagine, ignorance doesn't make very solid proof.

If someone is making the case for a particular view of the Millennium in Revelation 20 and I don't do a great job of disproving their view, they cannot think that is somehow evidence for their position. They have to promote their own position with a view that has fewer theological holes in it than my position. Their position has to stand on its own two feet by itself. You always have to support your own position; you cannot rely on the failures of others (to refute your position) as proof that it is right.

This fallacy happens a lot in politics. I saw a recent article that said that civilians carrying guns have never stopped a mass shooting. Therefore, citizens should not be allowed to carry guns.

Now, regardless of what you think about guns, the argument, itself, is flawed. First, it misses the point. The right to carry a gun for personal protection was not allowed at the federal or state level because the person had a legal obligation to stop a mass shooting. But, more importantly, every time a concealed carrier has shot a bad guy, the shooting doesn't continue and become a "mass shooting" because the suspect is dead! With this argument, the person is saying in effect: *When guns do stop a mass shooter, the shooting doesn't become a mass shooting and therefore guns have never stopped a mass shooting.* That is a strange argument indeed. But the fallacy here is that because we don't have evidence that carrying concealed handguns has stopped mass shootings, then they are obviously bad and could not stop a mass shooting. It is an example of the *ad ignorantiam* fallacy.

Misapplying the Analogy

If equivocation is the most common fallacy overall, this is the most common fallacy anytime someone uses an analogy. Misapplying the analogy is a type of category mistake.

Let's look at how analogies work. If I am describing what a donkey is and I say, "It is kind of like a horse," that does not mean it is *exactly* like a horse in every way. What this means is that there are only some ways in which a donkey is like a horse (it has four legs, it has a long snout, you can ride it, etc.). Analogies are meant to draw *at least* one similarity between two things, but you cannot draw all the similarities between them.

Please pause and hear this: There is no such thing as a perfect analogy. *If there was such a thing as a "perfect analogy," it would be the very thing it was being compared to.* If two different things are *exactly* the same in every way, then there is only one thing!

I say all that simply to say when someone is using an analogy, you have to ask yourself where the analogy is being drawn. When I am giving an analogy of a donkey being like a horse, I'm assuming that you will draw the analogy at the right place.

Let me give you an example. In the book of the Bible called Song of Solomon, the husband praises the beauty of his wife. In one line he says that her belly is like a "heap of wheat" (Song 7:2).

Now, where is the analogy being drawn? Is he saying her belly is huge and that she is out of shape? Is he saying that he can grind up her belly and make cereal out of it? Is he saying that her stomach is yellow in color?

Not at all!

Her belly is like a "heap of wheat" in the sense that wheat brings blessing and feeds mankind. Wheat is something we humans need for life and sustenance. *Her belly is a blessing.*

You see, if the writer's wife misapplies the analogy, then she will slap him in the face. But if she applies it in the right place, it all makes sense.

We even see analogies in the parables. In Luke 18 Jesus tells the story of a woman who bugs a mean judge until she gets justice. The point of the parable is not that God is mean or that he gets annoyed with us. It is that we are to be persistent in our requests to him.

Some people commit a similar fallacy even when an analogy is not being used. If someone were to say, "Hitler was a brilliant military strategist," that in no way means that they like Hitler or that Hitler was good or that they think we should have had Hitler as our leader. To assume that is to take one area (military strategy) and to read that onto another area (morality).

The bottom line is this: Anytime you are making an analogy, make sure people don't draw the analogy in the wrong place. Anytime someone else is making an analogy, make sure you draw the analogy at the right place.

Affirming the Consequent

Affirming the consequent has to do with how conditional sentences go together. A "conditional" is an "if/then" statement. For example, "If I don't drink water, then I will be thirsty."

The first part of the sentence (the "if") is called the antecedent (you can remember this because "ante" means "before"). The second part of the sentence (the "then") is called the consequent (you can remember this because the word *consequent* means something that follows something else).

However, we often misunderstand how if/then statements work. The affirming the consequent fallacy is when you say:

> If A, then B
>
> B
>
> Therefore, A

Notice that the structure only says that if A is true, then B will happen. But you cannot turn this around and say that if B is true then A must happen. That would be reversing the entire claim. That is a logical fallacy.

Let me show you what I mean by plugging in sentences for "A" and "B":

> "If I have bad breath, then people will not like me."
>
> "People do not like me."
>
> "Therefore, I must have bad breath."

But that's not necessarily true. I might have fresh minty breath and just be a total jerk. I might have the cleanest mouth in the world and be a really boring person. There are all kinds of reasons that people may not like me that are not dependent on my "if" statement above.

The "if/then" sentence only works when it stays in the correct order. I cannot affirm the "then" sentence (called the "consequent") and expect to get the same results.

Imagine seeing an advertisement for a gym that says, "If you don't work out, you will die at a young age." You then read the obituary of someone who died at the age of 21. You might conclude that they didn't work out. But that is a fallacy. There are a lot of other things that could have killed them (a grenade, getting stepped on by an elephant, etc.).

Or let's consider a theological example:

> If I am saved, then I will attempt to follow God's rules.
>
> I attempt to follow God's rules.
>
> Therefore, I'm saved.

But you see that this type of thinking is flawed. One follows God's rules as a result of God's free gift of salvation, not as a condition they must meet before God saves them. There are many people who try to be moral and attempt to follow God's rules who are not saved.

Anytime someone deals with a conditional (an if/then statement) and starts affirming the second part of that statement (the "then" clause), be careful that they are not affirming the consequent.

Denying the Antecedent

This is a similar fallacy to the previous one but from a different angle. The previous fallacy (affirming the consequent) meant affirming something incorrectly. This fallacy (denying the antecedent) means denying something incorrectly.

Denying the antecedent means that you have a conditional (again, a "conditional" is just a fancy term for an "if/then" sentence), and you deny the "if" part (the first part) of the conditional but expect the "then" part (the second part of the conditional) to also be denied.

This fallacy is demonstrated thus:

> If A, then B
>
> Not A
>
> Therefore, not B

That sounds technical, so let's look at a few examples:

> "If I have a great beach body, then all the women will want me."
>
> "I don't have a great beach body."
>
> "Therefore, all the women won't want me."

But this isn't true. Maybe I have a charming personality, a huge party yacht, or a sweet 401(k) that makes me irresistible to the ladies.

You see this mistake a lot in theology. For example, when it comes to forgiveness, I've heard people reason like this:

> "If someone asks for your forgiveness, then you should forgive them."
>
> "They didn't ask for your forgiveness."
>
> "Therefore, you should not forgive them."

But that is ludicrous. You are not allowed to withhold forgiveness just because someone doesn't come and apologize. Don't confuse your role with God's role. His forgiveness is linked to repentance. But our forgiveness for other humans is a command (regardless of what they do). "If your brother asks for forgiveness, then forgive them" does not logically imply if they don't ask for forgiveness then do not forgive them. That is the fallacy of denying the antecedent. God demands repentance for forgiveness, but he commands us to forgive regardless of whether the other person ever asks us for it.

Confusing "Is" and "Ought"

The philosopher David Hume pointed out that we cannot infer an "ought" (the way something should be) simply by observing an "is" (the way something *really* is). Those are two entirely different categories. This is what is known in philosophy as "Hume's guillotine." For example, let's say you see someone shoot another person. All you observed is the "is." Meaning, all you saw was someone shooting someone else. You did not *observe* whether it is "good" or "bad"—what is known as an "ought." You did not experience whether or not they *should have* shot them. You experienced an action; you did not experience a value judgment. Was it a murder and, in that case, something that "ought not" to have happened? Or was the shooting justified (perhaps the person being shot was threatening to kill a hostage), and in that case it "ought" to have happened? You don't know. To take Hume's point even further. Even if you knew that you witnessed a murder, you do not know it is "wrong" *just* by observing it. You have to read the category of "wrongness" (an "ought") back onto the situation from something you learned by way of ethics. You can't see "moral" and "immoral" through your five senses. All you can see is the "is" (the facts of what happened). You cannot see the "ought" (the moral weight of what happened). You learn "oughts" through the categories of ethics and theology.

This is a really esoteric way for me to simply say that *people often read judgment values onto something when all they have experienced is that thing itself.* When we see a tiger kill and eat another animal, we do not see whether that is "good" or "bad." To know the categories of good and bad, we need something other than our experiences. We need some standard of ethics.

A helpful contemporary example of this fallacy occurs in the argument that homosexuality is acceptable (an "ought") because it occurs among other animals in nature (an "is"). There are several problems with this line of thinking. First, some animals that perform a homosexual act later go on to breed with an animal of the opposite sex (thus destroying the idea that sexual orientation "cannot change"). Second, when we say that it is "natural" because it occurs in nature, we forget that nature is broken. Nothing is "natural" post-Genesis 3. Just because bad things happen in nature, that does not make them good. In nature mothers eat their young. In nature males rape females. In nature animals kill other animals for territory. It is a strange argument indeed to say that just because something happens, it "ought" to happen. This is where the confusing "is" and "ought" fallacy comes into play. People will say that just because homosexual acts occur in nature, they are therefore good. That is quite a leap. All you may see in nature, for example, is a male penguin performing a sexual act with another male penguin. You don't therefore see whether it is "good" or "ought" to be that way. That is something you have to infer from your worldview.

The bottom line is that we have to be careful when we are evaluating something we experience. *We have to distinguish between whether we are just describing something or whether we are ascribing a value to it.* Saying, "That man was killed," and saying, "Killing is bad," are two entirely different types of statements. One states a fact (an "is"), and the other states a value (an "ought").

The "After the Fact" Fallacy

We have all heard the phrase that "hindsight is 20/20." This fallacy is meant to help our *foresight* be closer to 20/20.

This fallacy judges the actions of someone based on information that they didn't have at the time—that only became available later.

To use a controversial, political example, consider "Operation Iraqi Freedom." In this military operation, Americans were sent into Iraq to prevent Saddam Hussein from developing "weapons of mass destruction" (WMDs). After the military operation was over, we didn't find weapons of mass destruction. Does that mean that overthrowing Saddam and going into Iraq was due to poor reasoning? If you think so, you may be committing the *after the fact* fallacy.

Now, don't get me wrong, I am not commenting either way on America's involvement in Iraq. That is a sticky topic (and God-loving Christians are free to disagree on this issue). The point of this example is to show that *if we had evidence that Saddam might have weapons of mass destruction, then that doesn't mean we necessarily made a logical mistake just because we didn't find any "after the fact."* The decision to go in had to be based on what might be the case, not what we were absolutely sure was the case. The evidence that we had at the time all pointed to Iraq possibly having WMDs. The fact that we didn't find any is irrelevant for answering the question "Should we have gone into Iraq based on the info we had at the time?" If you have evidence for something and you act on that evidence (and you are wrong), then you have indeed made a mistake—*but you have not acted unreasonably.* Now, you may say that we shouldn't have gone into Iraq for other reasons. Or you may say that the evidence we had did *not* point to Iraq possibly having WMDs. But the argument you cannot use is that we were wrong because we didn't find any WMDs *after the fact.*

You see this fallacy a lot in the media after there is a police shooting. News articles will often point out that someone who was shot by the police was "unarmed." But the fact that they turned out to be unarmed is irrelevant. *Were they acting like they were armed?* Were they being told to keep their hands where the police could see them, and they kept putting their hands in their pockets? Were the officers told by locals that the suspect had been seen with a weapon earlier? Did the suspect have a previous history of violent crime? Did the suspect rush the officer to potentially use the officer's own gun against them? *The officer cannot wait until the bad guy is actually shooting at them; it's too late then. Rather, they have to make the best call with the info they have at the time.* The "after the fact fallacy" assumes the officer was wrong based on info the officer didn't have when the shooting took place. Yes, it is sad anytime someone is shot. But it is also a shame when an officer is shot because he didn't act soon enough.

Notice that this is true in the shift between the Old Covenant and the New Covenant. Jews in the Old Testament are not expected to know who Jesus is because he has not come yet. They know a Messiah is coming, but they don't know when. But after Jesus comes, ignorance is no longer an excuse. Jews must believe in Jesus to be saved (e.g., John 3:18, Acts 4:12, Rom. 1:16). In the Old Testament pagan nations kind of went their own way. But in the New Testament, they are explicitly told that they must come to Jesus (Acts 17:30–31). God himself does not commit the "after the fact" fallacy. Now that the Messiah has come, ignorance is not excused.

In this fallacy, one confuses something that ends up being the case with the decisions people made when they did not have that info.

The Sorites Fallacy

This fallacy is named after what is called the "sorites paradox." What is this paradox?

Imagine that I take one grain of sand and ask you, "Is this a 'heap' of sand?"

You will probably say no. (We typically think of a "heap" of sand as something larger than one grain of sand.)

Now let's say I put two grains of sand together and ask the same question. Do you now have a heap of sand? You will again probably say no. Now let's say I keep adding one grain of sand at a time and asking the same question . . .

Here is what is tricky: At what point does it become a "heap" of sand? *If you don't know exactly how many grains of sand make a "heap," how will you ever know when you have enough sand to truly have a "heap"?* And yet, we all know a "heap" of sand when we see one! If we see a pile of sand, we would agree that it is a "heap" even if we don't know how many grains actually make a "heap."

Perhaps you arbitrarily say that for it to be a "heap" of sand, you have to have 100 grains of sand. I respond by asking, "So if I remove one grain of sand and you have 99 grains of sand, you would not count that as a heap? On what are you basing that idea?"

Now shake the sand out of your shorts and see this fallacy: The sorites fallacy means that someone acts as though just because you don't know *exactly* how many grains make a heap, you can't know what a heap is. But that is not always true.

Let me give three examples:

Imagine that a Baptist and a Methodist are talking about mode of baptism (how baptism should be done). Remember, Baptists think that baptism should be done by immersion, whereas a Methodist is okay with baptism being done by sprinkling or pouring. They might reason as follows:

> **Baptist:** Baptism should be done by dunking someone underwater.
>
> **Methodist:** But what if the top of someone's head doesn't fully go under the water? Have they not really been baptized? What if someone's hand comes out of the water? Have they not really been baptized? What if they are only halfway in the water in someone's bathtub? Does that count?
>
> **Methodist:** Therefore, the mode of baptism doesn't matter.

The error the Methodist has made in this example is the sorites fallacy. He is basically saying, "How many grains of sand make a heap?" or "How perfect does the immersion of the person have to be for it to be baptism?" But the Baptist was not claiming that the dunking had to be done perfectly. *He was simply claiming that an attempt should at least be made to fully immerse the person instead of intentionally trying not to immerse them with the mode of sprinkling.* The Methodist in this example is using the sorites fallacy to try to chip away at how much water really makes a baptism, but then jumps to the conclusion that we should *attempt a different mode of baptism* entirely (because we can't answer how many grains of sand make a heap—or how much water makes a baptism). This is not to give my opinion on mode of baptism, which I think is an important but secondary doctrine. There are good arguments to be made for using pouring or sprinkling in baptism; this is just not one of them.

Or consider the scenario where your teenage daughter wants to go hang out with her friends, and she wants to wear a skirt. You think that her skirt is too short, so she wants you to name exactly how long the skirt should be before you will let her wear it. You give her a number, and she says:

> "Are you really telling me that if I made it one millimeter shorter than the length you just told me, it would be inappropriate?"

Not only do you probably have a pretty smart daughter, but she has committed the sorites fallacy. *A dad can know his daughter's skirt is too short even if he doesn't know the exact mathematical length a skirt "should be."* There are general truths we can know even if we don't know all the particulars that make them up.

Or let's consider this scenario. The Bible commands us not to get drunk. But what does it mean to get "drunk"? We like to think that it is some governmental standard like a .08 blood alcohol level. But does that mean that if I blew into a breathalyzer (while in my home, not driving or in public) and it said I was .081 that I have sinned? What if it said .082? I might be declared "intoxicated" by a governmental definition but not by a biblical definition. Some people are perfectly lucid at .08, and others are falling on the floor. The Bible's definition is not a number, nor is it how good you feel, but whether or not the Spirit has ultimate control over you at that moment (or whether the alcohol has taken control according to Ephesians 5:18). But even though I don't know the "number" of drunkenness for every person (it is actually different for different people), that does not mean I don't know drunkenness when I see it. Now, I'm not advocating for you to break the law; please don't blow a .08 when you get pulled over on your way home from Chili's. I just want to point out that, sometimes, numerical standards commit the sorites fallacy.

You may be noticing a theme with this logical mistake. *Really the issue is that there are certain, definite categories of things (a heap, baptism, drunkenness, etc.), but the sorites fallacy tries to distract you from the categories to talk only about tiny parts.* It is a fallacy that appears to be a death by a thousand cuts.

In Genesis 18:22–33 Abraham is asking God to spare the city of Sodom and he keeps asking how many righteous people would need to be there to keep God from destroying it. God, will you spare the city for 45 people? How about for 40? How about for 30? 20? 10? Notice that Abraham is able to change the number, but the number never gets to zero. The point of the dialogue is how sinful Sodom is. There is not even a tiny remnant of righteous people. The number can change, but the fact that it doesn't go to zero means that the sorites fallacy has not been committed. We can debate what a "heap" is, but we know that zero grains of sand don't make a heap. Abraham can bring the number down, but he can't make the destruction of such an evil town go away.

But there is a right way to chip away at someone's argument. Asking about the parts of a category can be legitimate. It all depends on context. So be careful that you don't think that any example of breaking-things-down-into-tiny-parts is irrelevant. *Sometimes, you can show someone that they are reasoning incorrectly by using this technique against them.* It all depends on the actual claim someone is making.

The "In a Vacuum" Fallacy

This fallacy seeks to persuade people in one direction while ignoring a larger context or comparison of what is being claimed. It gives facts "in a vacuum" and ignores other relevant factors.

That definition was a little technical, so allow me to give some examples.

With the Coronavirus pandemic that began at the end of 2019 and shut down much of the US in 2020, the media produced an incredible hysteria by giving "facts" and "statistics" on how deadly COVID-19 was. Don't get me wrong; it is a bad disease and is especially dangerous to those who are older and have underlying medical conditions. Christians should make sure that they seek to care for their neighbors by seeking to limit the spread of the virus.

However, few people stopped to ask how deadly it was *compared* to anything else. After a year of COVID in the U.S., there were over 350,000 deaths. That sounds like a lot until you realize that, when not in a pandemic, 3 million Americans die every year. Worldwide there have been less than 2 million deaths in over a year of the pandemic. That's tragic, but we must remember that about 60 million people die worldwide every year from things other than COVID. Worldwide, about 161,000 people die every day. That means that more people die in 13 regular days than in over a year of COVID-19.

People were afraid to get the virus but forgot that about six million people get into car wrecks, just in the US, every year (any of which can be fatal). The virus had a death rate of under 1 percent in most places, whereas moderate to severe pneumonia has a death rate of 10 to 30 percent. Consider that 1.6 million people die from diarrhea each year, and we have all had that. This is not to say that precautions shouldn't have been taken. They should. This is not to say that the virus will not get worse (there will be many more deaths). But we also have to put it in *perspective* by not leaving these numbers "in a vacuum." People could have still acted in a way that is kind to their older neighbors without the fear and cowardice being promoted by the media.[8]

Notice, this has nothing to do with how deadly the disease is. If several years from now many more people have died, that wouldn't prove my point wrong. I am not saying it is a safe virus; *I am saying that the way the information was presented was biased and misleading.*

The same thing is true regarding the anti-vaccine movement mentioned earlier. Some people argue that putting certain chemicals and vaccines into your body is a bad idea. Others argue that children can have adverse reactions to vaccines. However, the question is not "Are some chemicals in vaccines bad for you?" Nor is the question "Do some people have adverse reactions to vaccines?" *The real question is, "Do vaccines cause more deaths than if we allowed deadly diseases to go unchecked by vaccines throughout the world?"* The anti-vaccine movement keeps the vaccine danger issue "in a vacuum" instead of asking whether the alternative (plague) is worse.

Or consider this example. Maybe you think guns are bad because they are a danger to children who can accidentally get a hold of one and fire it. But that argues "in a vacuum." According to the Center for Disease Control, about 69 children accidentally discharge a firearm in the US each year. (That is not how many die from such accidents; that is just how many accidentally fire a round.) But we have to put that in perspective. *More children die from bicycles each year than from firearms!* When you compare this with other factors, you see how clearly the "in a vacuum" fallacy errs in the way it presents data. Or, according to the FBI's annual report in 2011, 323 people were murdered with a rifle that year. That sounds like a lot, and you might be tempted to think the government should restrict owning rifles. But, in comparison, about 496 people that year were killed with hammers or clubs. *This means that blunt objects account for 60 percent more deaths than so-called assault rifles.*

So anytime someone makes a claim to try to persuade you in a particular direction, ask yourself, "What relevant factors or comparisons are they leaving out? How can I put this issue into perspective?"

Argument to the Absurd (*ad absurdum*)

With the *argumentum ad absurdum* fallacy, one appeals to what seems to be an absurd conclusion to an argument as a way to try to refute the actual argument.

However, this fallacy, like several of those described earlier, can be used in a way that is actually not fallacious.

Let me give you an example of both. First let's look at an example where the argument misfires.

Imagine that a Christian said, "Only people who know Christ will be saved." A skeptic might argue that "since this statement implies that most people are going to hell, and that seems absurd, then this statement is false."

Here the skeptic has committed the *ad absurdum* fallacy. A statement is not wrong *just because* it has an extreme conclusion. When I say, "All people alive today will eventually die," that is a true statement (assuming Christ doesn't return first) even though it has a pretty intense conclusion. Its conclusion *seems* absurd, but it is not actually absurd because it is exactly what will happen.

Someone commits this fallacy when they think that a conclusion is too extreme to stand with a particular statement, even though they can actually go together.

But there is a way in which the *ad absurdum* argument can be used as a rhetorical tool that doesn't commit any fallacies. It can be used to show that someone is being inconsistent with two opposing positions that they hold. Let's look at two examples:

First, if someone said that "any two people who love each other should be able to get married," you could ask the following questions:

> What about a brother and sister?
>
> What about a mother and son?
>
> What about a 60-year-old man and a 10-year-old boy?
>
> What about someone who has a secret family in Mexico and is trying to marry his girlfriend in the US?

In this example you are not actually committing a fallacy because *your questions challenge the actual logical implications of your opponent's original statement.* If their statement really is that the only thing required for marriage is that two people "love each other," then all these questions are fair critiques. If someone thinks that *any* two people who love each other should be able to get married, but a brother and sister who love each other should not, they have logically contradicted themselves, and the *ad absurdum* has helped point that out.

As a second example let's say that someone said, "Humans are just evolved apes on the same level as other animals." If I then responded and said, "That would mean that it is no more wrong to hunt a human than to hunt an animal," then I have used the *ad absurdum* argument *correctly*. Most people would agree that we cannot just kill people for sport. This conclusion should lead us to question whether the premise, "humans are just evolved apes on the same level as other animals," is actually true.

What the *ad absurdum* argument does it get you to go back and question your premise. Sometimes, you see that the conclusion is not absurd and is actually correct. But sometimes, the absurdity of the conclusion lets you see that you started with a faulty premise. This argument is meant to link the implications of one's statement with the actual statement itself (which then causes us to make sure we are being consistent with our worldview).

conclusion

I assume that this is probably one of the strangest books you have ever read. It moves from giving logical rules to ranting about theological issues to hammering social hot topics. Half the book is just pointing out flaws in the thinking of others. Some jokes were funny, and some were not. Some of my points you probably liked, and others you totally hated. Perhaps you thought that I was not taking logic seriously enough and didn't get into enough details, or perhaps you thought I was taking it too seriously. Maybe you're not a Christian and you think I have no idea what I'm talking about. Maybe you are a Christian and this is the first time you have realized how important it is to try to be right.

Why Be Logical?

There are many reasons we should try to be logical. First, it allows us to have confidence in what God has said in his word. An illogical interpretation is a wrong interpretation. Second, it honors God to think rightly on all topics. This isn't just true in theology.

God is honored when we think rightly in business, ethics, math, science, relationships, and any other field of inquiry. Third, it helps us challenge our views so we can repent of wrong ones. We are limited in our knowledge. This doesn't mean we can't know anything; it just means we can't know everything. Seeing the logical mistakes that we make helps us repent of unbiblical views. Fourth, it gives us confidence in what we do know. We don't have to just guess who is right on different views; we can actually see who is right. Fifth, it helps us teach, correct, and encourage one another. It makes our explanations of God and his word clearer. But there is an even bigger reason . . .

This book, for the Christian, all boils down to this: *We are to love God with all our mind, and we are to have correct doctrine.*[1] To do this we need to think well. In fact, the Bible commands us to be good thinkers and to have good theology:

> *But as for you, teach what accords with sound doctrine.*
> —Titus 2:1

> *In vain do they worship me, teaching as doctrines the commandments of men.*
> —Mark 7:7

> *We destroy arguments and every lofty opinion raised against the knowledge of God, and take every thought captive to obey Christ.*
> —2 Cor. 10:5

> *I appeal to you, brothers, to watch out for those who cause divisions and create obstacles contrary to the doctrine that you have been taught; avoid them.*
> —Rom. 16:17

So that we may no longer be children, tossed to and fro by the waves and carried about by every wind of doctrine.

—Eph. 4:14

My people are destroyed for lack of knowledge.

—Hosea 4:6

If you put these things before the brothers, you will be a good servant of Christ Jesus, being trained in the words of the faith and of the good doctrine that you have followed.

—1 Tim. 4:6

He must hold firm to the trustworthy word as taught, so that he may be able to give instruction in sound doctrine and also to rebuke those who contradict it.

—Titus 1:9

If you love me, you will keep my commandments.

—John 14:15

Loving God and being a good thinker go together. Not only is this true in the Bible; it is also true in church history. To be ordained a bishop in Egypt in the fourth century, one had to have all the Psalms, two of the major prophets (e.g., Isaiah and Jeremiah), all the Gospels, and all of Paul's letters completely memorized.[2] Jerome translated the entire Bible from Hebrew and Greek into Latin. Augustine was a rhetoric professor in Milan before his conversion and had a broad education in the humanities. He combined neo-Platonism with the Bible and wrote over five million words (that's the length of about 90 doctoral dissertations). He solved the problem of evil, defended the doctrine of grace, proved the existence of absolute truth, and defended the Trinity. In fact, he studied the Trinity for more than 22 years before he finished writing *De Trinitate.* Thomas Aquinas studied under Albert the Great in addition to attending the best university in the world at that time (the University of Paris). His *Summa Theologiae* is still one of the most influential theological textbooks ever. He was so smart that he could dictate three or four books to his scribes at the same time. He also wrote over eight million words (the equivalent length of about 144 doctoral dissertations).

Martin Luther had a doctorate in theology. He translated the entire New Testament from Greek into German in just 10 weeks by himself (while locked up in a castle struggling with spiritual attack). Luther thought that the biblical languages were so important that he said he would be willing to go to school with the devil to learn them. It is said that Luther encouraged Christians to study until they had taught the devil to death and had become more learned than God himself and all his saints. John Calvin studied at both the universities of Paris and Orleans and wrote one of the most popular Protestant systematic theology textbooks of all time. His first published book was a commentary on Cicero that he wrote in Latin at the age of just 23. Ulrich Zwingli, the "third man" of the Reformation, in addition to having a strong formal education, had all of Paul's letters memorized . . . in Greek.

George Whitfield and John Wesley both studied theology at Oxford. Jonathan Edwards went to Yale at 14, graduated with his bachelor's from Yale at 17 and had his master's from Yale before he was 20. He then went on to become the president of Princeton. He sometimes studied 14 hours a day and is considered to be the greatest mind to ever come out of North America. Charles

Spurgeon had a library of over 20,000 volumes and tutored Greek at Cambridge. He was reading the puritans by the age of 12.

But this isn't just true of church leaders from the past. It is also true of many church leaders today. John Piper has a D.Theol from the University of Munich. Wayne Grudem, who wrote a popular systematic theology textbook, has a bachelor's degree from Harvard, a master's degree from Westminster (which broke off from Princeton Seminary), and a PhD from Cambridge. N. T. Wright is considered to be one of the top New Testament scholars in the world; he has five degrees from Oxford, including two doctorates. Alister McGrath, the great historical theologian, has seven degrees from Oxford, including three doctorates. D. A. Carson, in addition to having a PhD from Cambridge, reads 500 books a year. Think about that . . . there are only 365 days in a year!

Now, these facts can seem overwhelming and discouraging.

This does not mean that you have to get a PhD in mathematical logic to be used by God. That is not my point. My goal is much more modest. My hope is that through all of this, just maybe, you have learned to be a better thinker. My hope is that there is at least one thing that stuck with you that you will use moving forward. This is a very short introduction to logic. Your journey has not ended. It has just begun.

notes

Chapter 1

1. If you want a good introduction to technical symbolic logic, I'd recommend Ernest Lepore, *Meaning and Argument: An Introduction to Logic Through Language*, 2nd ed. (Oxford: Wiley-Blackwell, 2009).

2. Molière, *Preface to Tartuffe*, in *Moliere's Writings about Tartuffe – Petitions to the King and Preface*, ed. R. W. Hartle (1965), https://pages.uoregon.edu/nateich/worldlit/moliere.html.

3. Irving M. Copi and Carl Cohen, *Introduction to Logic*, 12th ed. (New Jersey: Pearson, 2005), 4.

4. Patrick J. Hurley, *A Concise Introduction to Logic*, 10th ed. (Belmont: Thompson Wadsworth, 2008), 1.

5. Immanuel Kant, *Critique of Pure Reason*, trans. Werner Pluhar (Indianapolis: Hackett, 1996), 109.

6. D. Q. McInerny, *Being Logical: A Guide to Good Thinking* (New York: Random House, 2005), IX.

7. I know I ended this sentence with a preposition. But its alternative, "You don't have a right to your opinion. You only have a right for which you can argue," sounded really weird.

Chapter 2

1. Aristotle, *Metaphysics*, Book 4, trans. W. D. Ross (The Internet Classics Archive, MIT), http://classics.mit.edu/Aristotle/metaphysics.4.iv.html.

2. These two examples come from Lawrence Cahoone, *The Modern Intellectual Tradition: From Descartes to Derrida*. Audio Lectures. (Chantilly, VA: The Teaching Company, 2013).

3. St. Augustine is the one often credited for coming up with this line of reasoning.

4. Phillip Cary, *Good News for Anxious Christians: 10 Practical Things You Don't Have to Do* (Grand Rapids: Brazos, 2010), 115.

Chapter 4

1. When the Bible warns against philosophy in Colossians 2:8, it is not warning against studying what we think of as philosophy today (i.e., logic, ethics, politics, or reading someone like Plato). In fact, a warning against philosophy has to use philosophy to make a case for why you should avoid philosophy! Rather, by philosophy it means worldly thinking that is untrue and unbiblical. All true philosophy should be studied. A falsehood (what the text is actually warning against) is actually just poorly done philosophy.

Chapter 5

1. The points and information in this section came from three very helpful sources that discuss how we can speak about God:

- Thomas Aquinas, "Do We Have Words for God?" In *Aquinas: Selected Philosophical Writings, trans.* Timothy McDermott (Oxford: Oxford University Press, 2008).
- Thomas Williams, *Reason and Faith: Philosophy in the Middle Ages.* Audio Lectures. (Chantilly, VA: The Teaching Company, 2013).
- Frederick Copleston, *Medieval Philosophy: An Introduction.* (Mineola: Dover Publications, 2001).

2. Aseity means that God needs nothing. He has "of himself-ness." He is not like us. We are dependent on him, and he is self-existent and dependent on nothing.

3. John Calvin, *Institutes of the Christian Religion,* ed. John T. McNeill, trans. Ford Battles (Louisville, KY: Westminster John Knox Press, 2011), 121 (1.13.1).

Chapter 6

1. Lawrence Cahoone, *The Modern Intellectual Tradition: From Descartes to Derrida.* Audio Lectures. (Chantilly, VA: The Teaching Company, 2013).

Chapter 7

1. Just a reminder that the entire customary/imperial system is dumb, and we should have switched to the metric system a long time ago. It is, after all, more *logical.*

2. Inductive, Deductive, Deductive, Inductive, Deductive, respectively.

Chapter 8

1. Thankfully, the basic elements of logic have been used since Aristotle and are thus public domain (and do not require

citation). However, I have included here a list of helpful logic books from which I originally gleaned much of the material for this book as well as selected books I would recommend to others beginning to study logic:

- Irving M. Copi and Carl Cohen, *Introduction to Logic*, 12th ed. (New Jersey: Pearson, 2005).
- Patrick Hurley, *A Concise Introduction to Logic*, 10th ed. (Belmont: Thompson Wadsworth, 2008).
- Jack Sibly, *Logic for Life* (unpublished manuscript).
- Graham Priest, *Logic: A Very Short Introduction* (Oxford: Oxford University Press, 2000).
- Ernest Lepore, *Meaning and Argument: An Introduction to Logic Through Language*, 2nd ed. (Oxford: Wiley-Blackwell, 2009).
- Peter Kreeft, *Socratic Logic: A Logic Text Using Socratic Method, Platonic Questions, and Aristotelian Principles* (South Bend: St. Augustine's Press, 2010).
- Francis Howard-Snyder, *The Power of Logic*, 5th ed. (New York: McGraw-Hill, 2013).

2. I don't have a buddy named Ted, but you get the point. I just have to show them only one guy who is not sexist.

3. These rules are taken from Patrick Hurley, *A Concise Introduction to Logic*, 10th ed. (Belmont: Thompson Wadsworth, 2008).

Chapter 9

1. Several helpful insights in this chapter, especially the insights and examples for the Aristotle and Hume sections, were taken from Lawrence Cahoone, *The Modern Intellectual Tradition: From Descartes to Derrida,* Audio Lectures (The Teaching Company, 2013).

2. I wish we had time to explain Kant's critique of Hume, but that goes beyond the scope of this book.

Part II

1. It was silly for Martin Luther to call the book of James a "right strawy epistle" because he thought James didn't understand justification by faith as well as Paul. It is not James who misunderstands the gospel but Luther who misunderstands the idea of equivocation.

2. I don't like cats, which is why I used dogs for this example.

3. This is not an attempt to slander Dr. King. It is actually an attempt to show that we should listen to him in some areas, even when he is off in other areas. His adultery is well-known. But many do not know about his denial of the Trinity, the deity of Christ, and the resurrection. Joe Carter writes:

King held unorthodox views on theology, which he expressed during his time at Crozer Theological Seminary. In a paper he wrote for a systematic theology class he cast skeptical aspersions on the doctrines of divine Sonship, the Virgin Birth (". . . the evidence for the tenability of this doctrine is too shallow to convince any objective thinker"), and the Resurrection (". . . the external evidence for the authenticity of this doctrine is found wanting"). In the conclusion of another paper he writes, "Other doctrines such as a supernatural plan of salvation, the Trinity, the substitutionary theory of the atonement, and the second coming of Christ are all quite prominent in fundamentalist thinking. Such are the views of the fundamentalist and they reveal that he is opposed to theological adaptation to social and cultural change. He sees a progressive scientific age as a retrogressive spiritual age. Amid change all around he is willing to preserve certain ancient ideas even though they are contrary to science."

Joe Carter, "9 Things you Should Know about Martin Luther King, Jr." The Gospel Coalition, January 19, 2014, https://www.thegospelcoalition.org/article/9-things-you-should-know-about-martin-luther-king-jr-2/.

4. Yes, I know Leviticus 19:27–28 says not to tattoo your body, but (1) we are no longer under the Mosaic Law, (2) that text is about pagan practices (which is why it mentions making "cut marks on your body for the dead"), and (3) that exact passage also says you cannot trim your beard. So be consistent!

5. Roland Bainton, *Here I Stand: A Life of Martin Luther* (Peabody, MA: Hendrickson, 2009), 212.

6. *Terminus technicus* is a technical term in some field of study. It is an ironic phrase because terminus technicus is itself a terminus technicus!

7. Ryan Anderson, *When Harry Became Sally: Responding to the Transgender Moment* (New York: Encounter Books, 2018).

8. These numbers can be found with a simple Google search. Yes, the numbers could change, and yes, other articles might have slightly different numbers, but my point still stands. The fear level did not match the threat level with this disease.

Conclusion

1. A great book on this topic is J. P. Moreland, *Love Your God with All Your Mind: The Role of Reason in the Life of the Soul* (Colorado Springs: Navpress Publishing Group, 1997).

2. A special thanks to Michael Haykin for mentioning this in a lecture he gave on biblical interpretation in the fourth century at Reformed Theological Seminary.

CPSIA information can be obtained
at www.ICGtesting.com
Printed in the USA
BVHW040332130421
604736BV00008BA/1716